**JO EASTWOOD** is 100% British and lives in London. She is a painter, designer and traveller and once flew jet helicopters for a living. With her partner, Laurence Kemmish, she founded Gödel, Escher, Bach Ltd, an international marketing and management consultancy whose access to research data has made this book possible.

**TONY HUSBAND** has been a full-time cartoonist for four years and has worked for many national and specialist publications, including **Punch, Private Eye** and **Playboy,** (US). He was voted Joke Cartoonist of 1984 and 1985 and Strip Cartoonist for Yobs **(Private Eye)** in 1987. He has published a number of books and co-edits the popular national children's comic **Oink!,** which he co-founded with two others. Tony Husband has also written television comedy, designed greetings cards and worked in advertising. He is married and has a son.

GW00707371

# 100% BRITISH

## JO EASTWOOD

PENGUIN BOOKS
Published by the Penguin Group
27 Wrights Lane, London W8 5TZ, England
Viking Penguin, Inc., 40 West 23rd Street, New York, New York 10010, USA
Penguin Books Australia Ltd, Ringwood, Victoria, Australia
Penguin Books Canada Ltd, 2801 John Street, Markham, Ontario, Canada L3R 1B4
Penguin Books (NZ) Ltd, 182–190 Wairau Road, Auckland 10, New Zealand

Penguin Books Ltd, Registered Offices: Harmondsworth, Middlesex, England

First published 1988

Compilation copyright © Jo Eastwood, 1988

Cartoons copyright © Tony Husband 1988

All rights reserved.

To Javier Ergueta, who is
100% non-Brit...and who likes
it hot...

# CONTENTS

# INTRODUCTION

The nature of these survey results would lead the reader to believe that many percentages published here are a fabrication of the author. This is not the case.

All are drawn from authentic surveys conducted in Britain during the 1980s by polling and market research organizations, government offices and the Press. The majority of surveys took place in 1987.

The results explode a few myths about the image of the British and show their habits, opinions and attitudes to be at once contradictory, naïve, unbelievable, provocative, disturbing, outrageous or simply conformist.

The figures in brackets following each entry are reference numbers relating to each survey and a full list of these sources appears at the end of the work. The author has taken every measure possible to reproduce statistics in their original format so as not to risk changing their sense.

# ACKNOWLEDGEMENTS

This work could not have been produced without the (sometimes) involuntary contribution of many participants. In particular the author would like to thank Gallup, BMRB, MORI, NOP, OPCS, Marplan, Mintel, **The Times, Sunday Times, Financial Times, Guardian, Daily Telegraph**/Josie Heard, **Daily Mail, Mail on Sunday, Daily Express, Sunday Express, Independent, Today, She**/Dr David Delvin, **Woman**/Deirdre Sanders, **Woman's Own, Woman's World, General Household Survey, British Social Attitudes, Social Trends,** British Telecom and ROSPA. Thanks also to Apple Computer, whose user-promiscuous technology made compilation a simple and enjoyable process.

Personal thanks to my partner in life and work, Laurence Kemmish, for his encouragement and support, to my daughter and barometer, Miffy, for putting up with this rival for her attention, to the team of Gödel, Escher, Bach Ltd; Emma Wilson, Isobel Murray-Playfair, Fleur Young and Geoff Hunt.

But most of all my gratitude and appreciation go to my collaborator, Susan Jacks, who, during difficult times, displayed unfaltering stamina, commitment and enthusiasm. Without her assiduous hounding this book would have been neither possible nor on time.

# 1%

1% of Britons would prefer Margaret Thatcher to join them for Sunday lunch if they could choose a celebrity. (111)

1% of British adults suffer colic, head lice or ring worm in a 12-month period. (175)

1% of Britons most like Princess Michael as a member of the Royal Family...and the same amount prefer Prince Edward. (161)

1% of Britons would *least* like to receive a Christmas Day telephone call from...Colonel Gadaffi. (207)

1% of British men, while making love, *fantasize about their wife being responsive....* (238)

1% of British adults do not know whether they can ride a bicycle. (22)

**Britain's most wealthy** 1% of adults own 20% of all British marketable wealth. (261)

1% of British female youth feel that they might use hard drugs. (12)

**Less than** 1% of British deaths are attributable to suicide. (17)

1% of British pet owners have five or more dogs. (74)

1% of British women rode a horse in the four weeks prior to interview. (38)

1% of British men played cricket in the four weeks prior to interview. (38)

1% of British households have breakfast in the bedroom. (40)

1% of British households have dinner in the breakfast room. (40)

1% of British women, when asked what they most like about a man, say they are first attracted to his... money. (83)

1% of Britons believe they get the best cup of tea in...France. (109)

1% of British men, while making love, fantasize about having an extra large penis or several penises. (238)

13

**1.2%** of British households own a sailing boat. **(154)**

**1.3%** of British households own a camping vehicle or dormobile. **(154)**

**1.1%** of the British working population are in HM Forces. **(155)**

**1%** of the British population speak Flemish/Dutch. **(157)**

**1%** of British women smoke cigarillos. **(88)**

**1%** of British letter writers prefer their writing paper to be...black. **(176)**

**1%** of Britons suffer food allergies. **(181)**

**1%** of British cats live to be 21 years or more. **(188)**

**1% OF BRITISH WOMEN GIVEN SEXY LINGERIE BY A PARTNER WILL WEAR IT ONLY ON HIS BIRTHDAY. (150)**

## 1% OF BRITONS ADMIT TO PLAYING WITH TOY DUCKS IN THE BATH. (230)

1% of British women spent between £600 and £700 on clothes (outerwear) in the preceding year.(10)

1% of British spectacle wearers own more than three pairs of glasses. (110)

1% of British male partners do all the ironing in the home. (40)

1% of British male youth feel that they might have a homosexual relationship. (12)

1% of Britons believe that AIDS can be contracted through merely touching an infected person. (91)

1% of British women own a motorcycle over 125cc. (10)

1.5% of British employees work in the agriculture, forestry and fishing industries. (155)

1% of British ladies say they could never try cunnilingus. (105)

1% of British women say that their partner's smelly, sweaty feet annoy them most. (230)

1% of Britons believe the British winter begins between 1 and 14 September. (204)

# 2%

2% of British men keep a *chamber pot* in their bedroom. (230)

2% of Britons most like Prince Philip as a member of the Royal Family. (161)

2% of British households own an electric facial sauna. (10)

2% of British people feel that, as a form of protest, *seriously damaging government buildings,* should be allowed. (35)

2% of British home or garden accidents are caused by over-exertion. (232)

2% of British people do not know whether they own a motorcyle. (10)

2.7% of the British adult population is defined as Upper Middle Class, Social Grade A. (267)

2% of British male partners are mainly responsible for the cooking in the home. (40)

2% of British meals are stewed. (37)

2% of British men aged 18–44 suffered constipation in the previous month. (38)

2% of British people in Scotland and the North eat porridge for breakfast during the week. (40)

2% of British families with dependent children are headed by lone fathers. (51)

2% of British people would prefer Samantha Fox to join them for Sunday lunch if they could choose a celebrity. (111)

2% of British women would like their men to be...shorter. (83)

2.9% of British men use hair-colour restorers. (88)

2.9% of British women use hand-rolling tobacco. (306)

**Less than** 2% of British people wear contact lenses. (134)

2% of British men wear a hearing aid. (142)

**2% OF BRITISH PETS END UP IN BLACK BAGS THROWN IN
WITH THE RUBBISH...WHEN THEY ARE DEAD. (74)**

**2%** of British men choose gems for their women at Christmas to buy their way out of trouble. **(135)**

**2%** of British men who buy their partner's underwear, choose 'functional' outfits. **(150)**

**2%** of British people believe they get the best cup of tea in the...USA. **(109)**

**2.9%** of British women have black hair. **(88)**

**2%** of the British population in England and Wales are of Indian, Pakistani, Bangladeshi, Arab or mixed origin. **(120)**

**2%** of the British population speak Italian. **(157)**

**Only 2%** of British 41–45-year-old women would wear a mini skirt. **(172)**

**2%** of Midlanders think their passport photo makes them look...sexy. **(145)**

**2%** of British adults have a verruca in a 12-month period...and the same amount experience sunstroke.**(175)**

**2%** of British MPs find over 50% of the letters they receive 'difficult to understand'. **(177)**

**2%** of Britons would most like to telephone the Pope or Mr Gorbachov on Christmas Day. **(207)**

**2%** of British brides and bridegrooms plan to have more than four children. **(211)**

**2%** of British men, while making love, fantasize about dressing up in women's clothes...and 2% fantasize about making love with men. **(238)**

**An intrepid 2%** of British women claim to have had sexual feelings between the ages of one and five. **(105)**

**2%** of British households have an electric wafflemaker. **(40)**

**The cause of death of 2%** of British infants is attributed to accidents and violence. **(232)**

**2%** of British women say that poor dress sense turns them off most about the male sex. **(245)**

**2%** of British deaths of 40–44-year-olds are caused by cirrhosis of the liver. **(232)**

**2%** of British women call their romantic partners 'Honey Bun' or 'Honey Bunch'. **(246)**

**2%** of British women say they feel patronized when a man holds a door open for them. **(259)**

2% of British households contain six or more persons. (51)

2% of British women say they do knitting when they are supposed to be working...4% do crosswords and 22% make weekend and evening arrangements. (285)

2% of British women spent more than £700 on clothes (outerwear) in the preceding year. (10)

2% of British women say their men have no admirable qualities. (319)

2% of British adults made a will in a bank in the preceding 12 months. (29)

2% of British boys aged 14–15 ate three packets of crisps the day before interview and almost the same amount took a remedy for indigestion. (49)

**2% OF BRITISH WOMEN SAY THAT THEY HAVE HAD *MORE THAN 100 LOVERS IN A LIFETIME*. (105)**

# 3%

3% of British adults think that the Monarchy should be abolished. (227)

3% of British men have known a woman complain that his penis was too small. (238)

3% of British households own an electric footbath. (10)

3% of British female youth feel that they might have a lesbian relationship. (12)

3% of British male youth feel they might use hard drugs. (12)

3% of British 15–25-year-olds own stocks and shares. (12)

3% of British housewives serve Mulligatawny soup at least once every two to three weeks. (10)

3% of British people buy diesel cars. (52)

3.1% of British women have white hair. (88)

3% of British people think the Prime Minister has no influence on the country's future. (61)

3% of the British prison population are women. (76)

3% of British couples make love at least once a day...(82)

...and 3% of British women make love over 11 times each week. (105)

3.5% of British women are natural redheads; only 3% of Britain's eligible men like redheads. (88/342)

3% of British bridegrooms will be virgins on their wedding night. (118)

3.7% of British women own a knitting machine. (154)

3% of British people believe they get the best cup of tea in...Germany or Holland. (109)

Fewer than 3% of British company directors are women. (214)

3% of British women have asked to see their medical records. (115)

3% of British women who have defective eyesight do not wear glasses. (140)

3% of accidental fires in British households are first ignited with blowlamps. (136)

3% of British brides and bridegrooms use, or plan to use, no form of contraception...and 4.5% of them plan to have children right away. (211)

3% of British women describe their men as 'absolutely useless' between the sheets. (319)

**3.5% OF BRITISH MEN LIKE THEIR WOMEN TO WEAR PASSION KILLERS. (150)**

## 3% OF BRITISH WOMEN THINK THEIR MAN'S APPEARANCE IS...*APPALLING.* (97)

**3%** of British people who feel that a major nuclear accident in Britain is likely within the next ten years say that Britain should build *more* nuclear power stations. (35)

**Only 3%** of British bridegrooms are teenagers. (202)

**3%** of Britons would *least* like to receive a Christmas Day telephone call from...Arthur Scargill. (207)

**3%** of the British population speak Spanish. (157)

**3%** of British households do not have a television. (164)

**3%** of British people consider themselves belonging to the Poor social class. (127)

**3%** of English blood belongs to Group AB. (206)

**3%** of British adults suffer from sties in a 12-month period...and the same amount suffer boils, psoriasis and neuralgia. **(175)**

**3%** of British women say that their partner's snoring annoys them most. **(230)**

**3%** of British men say that their partner's daft habits – tapping fingers, biting and picking nails, the way they brush their teeth – annoy them most. **(230)**

**3%** of British women have tried 'wife swapping'. **(105)**

**3%–4%** of British skiers make medical insurance claims when they return home from their skiing holidays in the Alps. **(251)**

**3%** of British women say they would never attempt fellatio. **(105)**

**3%** of British households have a bidet. **(240)**

**3%** of British women think that Richard Gere has the best-looking body of all male personalities...3%

choose Mel Gibson and a further 3% choose Imran Khan. **(245)**

**3%** of British women think that Cliff Richard has the shapeliest bottom of all male personalities. **(245)**

**3%** of British men call their romantic partners 'Cuddles'. **(246)**

**3.4%** of the British population live in agricultural areas. **(268)**

**3.1%** of British adults own an allotment. **(154)**

**3%** of the British adult population are vegetarian. **(153)**

**3%** of the British working population work on Sundays. **(17)**

**3%** of British women say they bath once a week. **(286)**

**3.4%** of British women say they like tinkering with the car. **(307)**

**3%** of British men have a barometer or thermometer in their bedroom and 3% of British women keep a *chamber pot*. **(230)**

# 4%

4% of British readers of *Woman's Own* are...men. (125)

4% of British men buy toasters, vacuum cleaners or other household items for their women at Christmas. (135)

4% of British men buy gems for their women at Christmas to tell her that she's sexy. (135)

4% of victims of fatal accidents occurring in British homes are aged under five. (136)

4% of British adults believe that it is perfectly safe to take as many as they wish of medicines and treatments that can be bought. (175)

4% of British men who have difficulty with eyesight do not wear glasses. (140)

4.3% of British households own a caravan. (154)

4% of British women think that Tom Selleck is the most attractive man in the public eye. (245)

Only 4% of Britons eligible to donate their blood do so. (206)

4% of Britons, when asked who they would most like to telephone on Christmas Day, choose...Margaret Thatcher. (207)

4% of Britons, if given the opportunity to make a Christmas Day telephone call that would change the world, would ring God. (207)

4% of Britons met the love of their life in March. (204)

4% of British men keep a candle in their bedroom. (230)

Only 4% of Britons say they are not very happy with their spouse. (230)

4% of British married and single men consider themselves bisexual. (238)

4% of British brides proposed to their fiancé. (118)

4% of Britons drink beer for lunch on weekdays. (285)

4% of Britons most like Prince Andrew as a member of the Royal Family. (161)

4% of British AIDS victims are female. (17)

4% of Britons sleep while they bathe. (230)

4% of British domestic accidents occur in the bathroom/lavatory. (232)

4% of British people own a motorcycle. (10)

4% of British adults claim to be underweight. (175)

4.2% of British couples divorce after 30 years of marriage. (17)

4% of British women played darts in the four weeks prior to interview. (38)

**4% OF BRITISH MEN CONSIDER A HAMMOCK TO BE THE MOST ROMANTIC HONEYMOON BED. (246)**

**4%** of British men went fishing in the four weeks prior to interview. **(38)**

**4.5%** of British readers of *Successful Slimming* magazine are heavy users of sausages. **(88)**

**4%** of British companies put a total ban on accepting gifts. **(43)**

**4%** of British adults find their weekends lonely. **(60)**

**4%** of British women have taken part in an 'orgy'. **(104)**

**4%** of British people feel that not getting along with relatives is sufficient reason for divorce. **(35)**

**4%** of British people think the 'City' has no influence on the country's future. **(61)**

**4%** of British wives in full-time employment work longer hours than their husbands. **(64)**

**4%** of British young women aged 15-34 believe they can catch AIDS from a toilet seat. **(76)**

**4%** of British couples say they would never try making love in the bath and the same amount say they don't like making love in the kitchen either. **(105)**

**4.3%** of the British population is non-white. **(266)**

# 5%

5% of British 15–25-year-old females feel that they might shoplift. **(12)**

5% of British households own a budgie. **(18)**

5% of British women think that 'Fergie', Duchess of York, is the most stunning woman in the public eye. **(245)**

5% of British women aged 18–24 are heavy drinkers of alcohol. **(38)**

5% of British people say they know a lot about wine. **(41)**

**Only 5%** of British women would like to strip Dirty Den of his tie. **(272)**

5% of British people would *least* like to see Prince Charles if a member of the Royal Family were to come to their area. **(163)**

5% of British household members do not eat breakfast during the week. **(40)**

5% of British household members eat sausages for breakfast during the weekend. **(40)**

**5.6%** of British women do not use shampoo.**(88)**

5% of British housewives are heavy users of suet. **(88)**

5% of British women think their hips are their best feature. **(107)**

**5.2%** of mail delivered in the United Kingdom consists of greeting cards. **(121)**

5% of fatal accidents occurring in British homes are due to burns. **(136)**

5% of British women have a hangover in a two-week period. **(143)**

5% of British men and women prefer to kiss in the dark. **(89)**

5% of accidental, non-fatal poisoning cases in British homes are caused by rat and mouse poison. **(136)**

**5.1%** of the population of Great Britain live in Wales. **(156)**

# I'm sorry, dear....

## 5% OF BRITISH MEN MAKE THE FIRST MOVE TO RECONCILIATION AFTER LOSING THEIR TEMPER. (102)

**5%** of British children suffer nappy rash. (175)

**5%** of Britons who buy or rent videos have *never* been to a cinema. (205)

**5%** of Britons would *least* like to receive a Christmas Day telephone call from...the police. (207)

**5.1%** of British people prefer the word 'briefs' to 'knickers' as a term of reference. (150)

**Only 5%** of British people spend over £6 on a pair of knickers. (150)

**5%** of British teachers say that they have been physically attacked by a parent. (169)

5% of British adults smoke cigars or pipes. (175)

5% of British couples go to the West Indies for their honeymoon. (211)

5% of British women learnt the 'facts of life' from their father. (105)

Only 5% of British women would like to have a bigger bust. (229)

5% of British women think it is wrong to masturbate these days. (105)

5% of British men fantasize about being raped by a woman or women...and a further 5% fantasize about making love with an actress, sportswoman or TV personality. (238)

5% of British women are lesbian. (105)

5% of British 16–24-year-olds share a toothbrush with their spouse, family or partner. (243)

5% of British households have an electric carving knife. (255)

5% of Britons aged 35–50 say they met their present partner on the street. (301)

5% of British women say they have problems with plumbing. (286)

5% of British men and women say they first made love to their partner in the open air. (301)

5% of British women think that Tom Selleck has the most handsome face and the shapeliest legs of all male personalities...only 3% vote for his bottom. (245)

5% of British males with AIDS are haemophiliacs. (263)

5% of British women think that Cliff Richard has the best head of hair of all male personalities. (245)

5% of British women think of feminists as extremists. (250)

Britain's most wealthy 5% of adults own 40% of all Britain's marketable wealth. (261)

5% of British women say that it is a man's hips that most turns them on...4% go for the hands. (287)

5% of British men say they mainly talk about hobbies, i.e. knitting, while they are at work. (285)

5% of British couples keep their own money separate. (35)

5% of British men buy jewellery for a woman to tell her that they feel guilty about neglecting her. (135)

# 6%

6% of British women *do not know* whether they reach a climax during intercourse. (105)

6% of British households own an electric styling wand. (10)

6% of British 15–25-year-old males worry a lot about being attacked at night. (12)

6% of British men suffer depression. (38)

6% of British girls claim to be vegetarian. (12)

6% of British men rate shopping as an enjoyable activity. (30)

6% of British men played football in the four weeks prior to interview. (38)

6% of British women say they have made love in a 'threesome', with a woman and a man. (105)

6% of British women say they dislike 'saying naughty things' to their partner in bed. (105)

6% of British adults suffer from travel sickness in a 12-month period and the same amount experience...warts. (175)

6% of British letter writers throw away letters immediately after receiving them. (176)

6% of British women say that body-builder-type muscles turn them off most about the male sex. (245)

6% of British dogs are 'put to sleep' because of anti-social behaviour. (188)

6% of Britons do not know when winter officially begins. (204)

6% of Britons say that in the last 12 months they have driven four or more times while 'over the limit'. (208)

6% of Britons say they feel 'quite violent' after watching certain television programmes. (218)

6% of British 15–25-year-olds worry a lot about whether to sleep with their girl or boyfriend. (12)

6% of British households have red kitchens. (40)

6% of British households claim to eat in the kitchen. (40)

6% of British couples argue about money most at weekends. (60)

6% of British housewives do not use toothbrushes. (88)

6% of British women use the coil as a means of contraception. (107)

6% of British men wear designer labels. (97)

6% of British couples have made love on a waterbed. (105)

6% of British women can't stand their work. (107)

My Wife's Anorexic

**6% OF BRITISH WOMEN HAVE HAD ANOREXIA. (107)**

6% of British viewers vote Jonathan Ross the best chat-show host. (119)

6.5% of British viewers operate a TV set without a licence. (335)

Of the six million accident cases seen by hospital casualty departments each year in Britain, 6% occur in schools. (136)

6% of British husbands take the kids to school. (230)

6% of British women think that Cliff Richard is the best-dressed of all male personalities. (245)

6% of British women think that 'Fergie', Duchess of York, is the best-dressed of all the female royal personalities...and a further 6% choose the Queen. (245)

6% of British women have never smacked their children. (255)

For 6% of Britons, cycling is the main mode of transport...and a further 6% walk. (263)

6% of Britain's Asian population speak mainly English at home. (275)

6% of British women keep a candle in their bedroom. (230)

6% of British women say they have never experienced a sexual climax. (105)

6% of homicide cases in England and Wales are committed in furtherance of theft or gain. (265)

6% of Britons say they are late for work almost every day. (285)

Only 6% of British workers have photographs of their families at their place of work. (285)

6% of British men say they mainly talk about girlfriends and women when they are at work. (285)

6% of Britons aged 35–50 say they met their present partner on a blind date. (288)

6% of British men say that sexually explicit scenes should not be shown on television at any time...14% of women agree. (288)

6% of Britons say that only effeminate men wear aftershave. (307)

# 7%

7% of British adults suffer from ingrown toenails in a 12-month period. (175)

7% of British schoolchildren admit to stealing. (302)

7% of British women think that Jeffrey Archer has the best-looking body of all male politicians. (245)

7% of British adults consider *colour scheme* to be most important factor when buying a bicycle. (22)

7% of all British pupils go to private schools. (35)

7% of British boys of all ages smoke regularly. (38)

7% of British men over 18 years are underweight. (38)

7% of British people with literacy problems cannot read or write at all. (36)

7% of British couples do 'something else' after going to bed but before falling asleep on Saturday nights. (60)

Only 7% of British families make conversation during Sunday lunch. (62)

7% of British females wash their hair once a day or more. (73)

7% of the British population who read the *Financial Times*...are aged 15–19 years. (78)

7% of British women say they have made love in a threesome, with two men. (105)

Only 7% of British women in Wales say their men are ideal. (83)

7% of British women say their men's bodies embarrass them. (90)

7.5% of the UK victims of accidental drowning in 1987 died in cars; 6.7% drowned while boating. (329)

7% of British men do not use shampoo. (88)

7% of British adults have a bank loan. (138)

**7.7%** of British people prefer the word 'undies' to 'knickers' as a term of reference. **(150)**

**7%** of British people are in various stages of getting dressed when they have breakfast. **(160)**

**7%** of British people would *least* like to see Prince Philip if a member of the Royal Family were to come to their area..and the same amount would least like to see the Princess of Wales and the Duchess of York. **(163)**

**7%** of British letter writers prefer pink writing paper. **(176)**

**7%** of British adults have bought wine to lay down. **(41)**

**Only 7.8%** of British high earners regularly attend a concert, the theatre or a cinema. **(56)**

**Only 7%** of British men say they go to pubs for 'chatting up' purposes. **(198)**

**7%** of Britons say they met the love of their life in December. **(204)**

**7%** of British bridegrooms proposed...in the car. **(211)**

**7%** of British men, while making love, fantasize about bondage and being dominated by their partner or an older woman. **(238)**

**7%** of British married men have had a romantic friendship with another male. **(238)**

**7%** of British men prefer to watch TV when they are with their partner. **(246)**

**7%** of the British share-owning population own shares only in companies that have been privatized. **(263)**

**7%** of British women would like to strangle Terry Wogan with his own tie...and 7% would like to undo his tie and top shirt button. **(272)**

**7%** of Britain's ethnic minorities are Sikh. **(275)**

**7%** of British households have a dishwasher. **(303)**

**7%** of British men use an after-bath moisturizer. **(90)**

**7.5%** of Britons agree that a *real man* can down several pints of beer at a sitting. **(307)**

**7.3%** of British men say that expensive perfume is something they can't resist. **(307)**

**7%** of British women regard their kitchen as a room to play in. **(40)**

# 8%

8% of British women have over 11 orgasms each week. (105)

8% of British men keep a cross or other religious symbol in their bedroom. (230)

8% of British people most like Princess Diana as a member of the Royal Family. (161)

8% of British women claim that they are always overdrawn at the bank. (114)

8% of British 15–25-year-old males own stocks and shares. (12)

8% of British 15–25-year-old females think that a woman's place is in the home. (12)

8% of British housewives say their husbands are 'absolutely hopeless' at cooking. (37)

8.2% of British males over 18 years are obese. (38)

8% of British women have trouble sleeping. (107)

8% of British males use hairspray. (71)

8.9% of British couples divorce within two years of marriage. (17)

8% of British adults do not know how to ride a bicycle. (22)

8% of British people think coffee is the most relaxing drink at bedtime. (109)

8% of British 16-year-old-boys receive £10 a week or more pocket money. (49)

8.7% of British high earners go jogging. (56)

8% of British women suffer from depression frequently. (107)

8% of British people take milk for a hangover cure. (108)

8% of British households have a burglar alarm. (113)

8% of British viewers vote Clive James the best chat-show host. (119)

## 8% OF BRITISH MEN WOULD ASK THEIR WOMEN TO REMOVE A SPIDER FROM THE BATH. (99)

**8.5%** of British adults have brewed beer at home in the last 12 months. **(88)**

**Only 8%** of British people expect unemployment to have gone down in a year from now (1986). **(35)**

**8%** of British men who wear glasses still have defective eyesight. **(140)**

**8%** of British MPs prefer to receive handwritten letters. **(177)**

**8%** of British dwellings are bungalows. **(139)**

**8.35%** of British nurses are male. **(271)**

**8%** of homicide cases in England and Wales involve the use of a firearm. **(265)**

**8%** of Britons say they mainly talk about television and soap operas when they are at work. **(285)**

**Only 8%** of British workers say they eat crisps for lunch. **(285)**

**8.5%** of British housewives do not use toothpaste. **(88)**

**8%** of fatal accidents occurring in British homes are due to suffocation and choking. **(136)**

**8%** of fatal accidents occurring in British homes are due to conflagration. **(136)**

**8%** of British adults suffer denture problems in a 12-month period. **(175)**

**8%** of Britons take their home holidays by the rivers and lakes. **(162)**

**8%** of British women say they would never try 'saying naughty things' to their partner in bed. **(105)**

**8%** of British men, both married and single, say they have regularly enjoyed cross-dressing. **(238)**

**8%** of British men keep photographs of their wedding in their bedroom...9% of British women do so. **(230)**

**8%** of British women say that Mike Baldwin of 'Coronation Street' deserves the title 'Romantic Rat of the Year'. **(246)**

**8%** of deaths of 30–34-year-olds in Britain are caused by heart disease. **(232)**

**8%** of defendants in England and Wales proceeded against at magistrates' courts for motoring offences are aged 10–17 years. **(265)**

**Only 8%** of British 18-year-olds attempt GCE A-levels. **(269)**

# 9%

9% of British men keep a musical instrument in their bedroom. (230)

9% of British women use the diaphragm for contraceptive purposes. (107)

9% of British women are not at all satisfied with their kitchen. (40)

9% of British women say their kitchen is a room to relax in. (40)

9% of British people take, for a hangover cure,...more alcohol. (108)

9.8% of British schoolgirls leave school with no GCE or CSE grades. (42)

9% of British women say they are first attracted to a man's looks. (83)

9% of British people say they get the best cup of coffee in Italy. (109)

9.9% of British women are natural blondes. (88)

9% of British women make love five times each week. (105)

9% of British men take their shirt or vest off last when undressing. (90)

9% of British householders are not concerned about home safety and security. (113)

9% of British people think that scientists, as a breed, are irresponsible. (117)

9% of British top earners (£25,000+ annual household income) have a second home. (56)

9% of British adults feel that they have moved into a lower social class compared with their parents. (127)

9% of British people are seen by hospital casualty departments each year following accidents. (136)

9.7% of the British working population are self-employed. (155)

9.3% of the population of Great Britain live in Scotland. (156)

9% of the British population speak German. (157)

9% of British people most like the Duchess of York as a member of the Royal Family. **(161)**

9% of British people would most like to see Princess Anne if a member of the Royal Family were to come to their area. **(163)**

9% of British women say their men have hit them after arguments about the children. **(319)**

9% of British women think that Victoria Principal has the shapeliest bottom of all female personalities. **(245)**

9% of British men, while making love, fantasize about making love to two or more women. **(238)**

BEWARE OF THE DOG

**9% OF BRITISH ADULTS RUN OR JOG...AND THE SAME AMOUNT SUFFER ATHLETE'S FOOT AND ANIMAL BITES IN A 12-MONTH PERIOD. (175)**

**9%** of Britons own shares in British Gas. **(263)**

**9%** of robbery offences in England and Wales involve the use of a firearm. **(265)**

**9%** of British women think that David Steel has the best-looking body of all male politicians. **(245)**

**9%** of British cats have a pedigree. **(188)**

**9%** of English blood belongs to Group B. **(206)**

**9%** of British people read in the bath. **(230)**

**9%** of British adults suffered from varicose veins in the last 12 months. **(306)**

**9%** of British women say that sex is the most important aspect of their relationship with their man. **(112)**

**9%** of Britons would *least* like to receive a Christmas Day telephone call from...the taxman. **(207)**

**9%** of British couples use a horse and carriage to transport them on their wedding day. **(211)**

**9%** of Britons take sleeping pills or tranquillizers before going to bed. **(230)**

## 10% OF BRITISH PET FISH GET NEW HOMES FOR CHRISTMAS. (50)

# 10%

10% of British people say they feel embarrassed or self-conscious wearing glasses. (134)

10% of British men have defective colour vision. (141)

10% of British women prefer their men to wear *nothing* beneath their jeans. (150)

10% of the causes of accidental fires in British households are deliberate or possibly deliberate. (136)

10% of British women avoid the sun. (107)

10% of British people feel that there should be no private schools at all. (35)

10% of British people would *least* like to see Princess Margaret if a member of the Royal Family were to come to their area. (163)

10% of British women think that Princess Anne has the best-looking body of all female royal personalities. (245)

10% of British adults suffer from hayfever and haemorrhoids in a 12-month period. (175)

**Only** 10% of British brides are teenagers. (202)

10% of British motorists have lost a friend or relative in a drink-related accident. (208)

*At least* 10% of London cabbies have A-levels. (216)

10% of British marriages are on the verge of collapse. (222)

10% of British adolescents think that the Monarchy should be abolished. (227)

10% of British men say that their partner's nagging and nattering annoys them most. (230)

**Only** 10% of British men who have been sexually harassed or assaulted say that it was by a woman. (238)

10% of British women say that they have been raped. (105)

10% of British women think that Princess Michael of Kent has the most attractive face of all female royal personalities. (245)

10% of British men usually send *rude* Valentine's cards...and 10% receive them. (246)

10% of British women would most like to spend Valentine's Day with Terry Wogan. (246)

10% of British women say they don't like sex; 10% say their men are bores. (319)

10% of British women aged 21–30 say they feel either no different or depressed after making love. (250)

10% of British domestic accidents occur in the bedroom. (232)

10% of British women say that they would mind if their child married someone of a higher social class. (255)

**Nearly** 10% of the British population now has private medical insurance. (263)

10% of persons found guilty of, or cautioned for, burglary offences in England and Wales are aged 10–13 years. (265)

10.3% of British employees work in banking, insurance and finance. (155)

10% of the British police force are women. (270)

10% of British women would like to have a red kitchen...and 10% would like a grey one. (40/273)

10% of British housewives clean the kitchen floor every day. (273)

10% of British men say they mainly talk about politics while they are at work. (285)

10% of the complaints by British women regarding harassment in offices concern physical assault. (316)

10% of British men still seem to be dominated by their parents. (112)

10% of British males suffer serious impotence. (11)

10% of British housholds consist of men living alone. (3)

10% of British consumers complain that retail staff are patronizing and condescending. (7)

10% of British people purchased cod liver oil tablets in the preceding year. (10)

10% of deaths of one–four-year-olds in Britain are caused by cancer. (232)

10% of British women have asked their doctor for an abortion and of these 10% had a GP who refused to help. (115)

10% of British married couples were childhood sweethearts. (118)

10.4% of British high earners take part in voluntary and charity work. (56)

10% of British men think that women are *more* attractive in spectacles. (110)

10% of Scottish men conveniently forget to pay back money borrowed from a friend. (86)

10% of British 15–19-year-old males rate money first above health. (12)

10% of British women over 18 years eat chips on most days. (38)

10% of British households in Wales and the South West serve Scotch Broth at least once every two to three weeks. (40)

10.9% of British women aged 18–44 suffered constipation in the previous month. (38)

10% of Britain's 'eligible' men say they do not care about a woman's bra size. (342)

**10% OF PEOPLE IN BRITAIN SPEND PART OF THEIR LIFE IN A MENTAL HOSPITAL (69)**

# 11%

11% of British people would rather hop into bed with someone special in order to keep warm than don an extra sweater or have a double brandy. **(47)**

11% of British men wash their hair once a day...or more. **(73)**

**11.7%** of the British adult working population are unemployed. **(77)**

11% of British men get embarrassed at watching on-screen sex. **(85)**

11% of British men ask their partners to 'go Dutch' on their birthday dinner treat. **(86)**

11% of British women say their men are 'downright mean'. **(86)**

**11.4%** of British adults use remedies for haemorrhoids. **(88)**

11% of British women think their men have no dress sense whatsoever. **(97)**

11% of British men have had a vasectomy. **(104)**

11% of drownings in Britain occur in the bathtub. **(232)**

11% of British men say they have been sexually harassed... **(238)**

11% of British 15–25-year-old females feel they might smash things up when angry. **(12)**

11% of British Airways' business travellers are women. **(31)**

**Only** 11% of British women say they never see a doctor. **(38)**

11% of British women over 35 years use computer dating, blind dates or personal ads in order to meet men. **(112)**

11% of British men would not stand up for a lady's honour if a stranger became abusive. **(48)**

11% of British drivers have defective eyesight. **(134)**

11% of British women who have defective hearing do not wear an aid. **(142)**

11% of British husbands with sexual difficulties say the problem is their lack of interest in sex. (238)

**Only** 11% of British people fear that their earnings may fall after the stock market collapse in October 1987. (130)

11% of all fatal accidents occurring in British homes are due to poisoning. (136)

11% of British people feel that private medical treatment in all hospitals should be abolished. (35)

11% of Welsh couples go to Spain for their honeymoon. (118)

11% of British people support the construction of more nuclear power stations. (35)

11% of British people would most like to see the Queen Mother if a member of the Royal Family were to come to their area. (163)

11% of British nurses have been physically injured by patients over the last year. (192)

11% of Britons who buy or rent videos have *never* bought a book. (205)

11% of British women keep a cross or other religious symbol in their bedroom....while 11% of British men keep a weapon in their sleeping quarters. (230)

11% of British men, while making love, fantasize about their partner wearing stockings and suspenders, high-heels, leather, rubber and uniforms. (238)

**Only** 11% of British young women say they are talked into having intercourse the first time. (238)

11% of British husbands who have had affairs say they do not know with how many women they have been unfaithful. (238)

11% of British divorced men do not want to remarry. (238)

11.3% of British housewives use birdseed. (88)

11% of British men have suffered from a sexually transmitted disease or infection. (238)

11% of British women dislike fellatio...and the same amount say they would never try making love in the kitchen. (105)

11% of British men would like to spend Valentine's Day with Anneka Rice...and 11% of British women would like to spend it with Nick Owen. (246)

11% of British women say their men are too rough and selfish to make sex enjoyable. (319)

11% of British women think that Joan Collins is the most stunning woman in the public eye. (245)

For 11% of Britons the bus is the main mode of transport. (263)

11% of Britain's ethnic minorities are Hindu. (275)

11% of British men say that they write personal letters when they are supposed to be working. (285)

11% of Britons aged 35–50 met their present partner at the office during working hours. (288)

11.1% of British adults take tonics. (88)

11% of Britons say that food does not interest them. (307)

11% of British households own a rechargeable shaver. (10)

**Only 11%** of British women ask their partner if they may borrow their razor before shaving their legs. (1)

11% of reported sexual harassers in British offices are relocated...22% are warned by management...and 20% get away with it. (316)

**12% OF BRITISH PEOPLE KISS THEIR FRIENDS ON THE LIPS. (89)**

# 12%

12% of British fish owners believe their *pet knows it's Christmas.* (50)

12% of British women say they would never try making love in front of a mirror. (105)

12% of British adults have a personal loan/overdraft at a bank. (29)

Only 12% of adults in Britain have ever hired a car. (34)

12% of British households own a wok. (37)

12.3% of British women use hair bleaches and lighteners. (88)

12% of British housewives consider canned food very healthy. (37)

12% of British women have made love in unusual clothing...leather, plastic boots, etc. (105)

12% of British women knit before dinner. (230)

12% of British girls of all ages smoke regularly. (38)

12% of British adults who drink alcohol drink gin regularly. (41)

Only 12% of British high earners spend time on physical activities. (56)

12% of British women think their men are fairly secretive. (87)

12.2% of British readers of 'Men Only' magazine...are women. (306)

12% of British men are shy about walking around the bedroom naked. (90)

12.5% of British women describe their GPs as 'dedicated beyond the call of duty'. (115)

12% of British viewers vote Michael Parkinson the best chat-show host. (119)

12% of male employees in Great Britain work over 50 hours a week. (17)

12% of British nurses work between five and ten hours overtime a week. (133)

**12%** of Britons think of crime and danger when they hear the term 'inner cities'....11% think of dirt...**(320)**

**12%** of victims of fatal accidents occurring in British homes are aged 15–44. **(136)**

**Only 12%** of British women think their man looks macho in his underwear. **(150)**

**12.3%** of the population of Great Britain are resident in Greater London. **(157)**

**12%** of the British population are Roman Catholic. **(157)**

**Only 12%** of Britons consider national newspaper journalists to be trustworthy. **(313)**

**12%** of British men report literacy problems since leaving school. **(36)**

**12.8%** of British schoolboys leave school with no GCE or CSE grades. **(42)**

**12%** of Britons buy their stockings

from Marks & Spencer. **(183)**

**12%** of British nurses plan to quit because of bad backs. **(192)**

**12%** of British men now in their forties had sexual intercourse while under 16 years of age. **(238)**

**12%** of British men say that either they have made sexual advances towards a member of their own family or that a member of the family has made advances towards them. **(238)**

**12%** of British women think that Adam Carrington of 'Dynasty' deserves the title 'Romantic Rat of the Year'. **(246)**

**12%** of firearm offences in England and Wales involve the use of a long-barrelled or sawn-off shotgun. **(265)**

**12%** of the British working population are engaged in shift work. **(17)**

**12%** of British men wake before 5.30 a.m. on weekdays...6% of women do so. **(285)**

# 13%

13% of British people believe that Prince Charles should not speak out on controversial issues. (161)

13% of British people feel that Britain would be better off without the Royals. (161)

13% of British adults suffer hair loss and baldness in a 12-month period. (175)

13% of Britons take their home holidays on the moors and in the mountains. (162)

13% of British men, while making love, fantasize about making love on beaches, in forests and in mirrored rooms. (238)

Only 13% of British drivers involved in accidents are breathalysed. (187)

13% of British cats 'choose their owners'. (188)

Of the 13% of Britons who think they know the name of their Euro MP, 5% get it wrong. (190)

13% of British women think that David Owen has the nicest personality of all male politicians. (245)

13% of Britons say they take between 60 and 74 minutes for lunch on weekdays. (285)

13% of British men under 24 say they think more highly of non-virgins. (287)

13% of British DIY consumers are classified as 'Reluctant Ronnies'. (308)

13% of British women think a beard on a man is sexy. (1)

13% of British women make love between six and ten times each week. (105)

13% of British households own a gas-powered styling brush. (10)

13% of British 15–25-year-old males feel that they might shoplift. (12)

13% of Britons condemn thermal underwear as 'unwearable'. (150)

**13% OF BRITISH WOMEN WHO WEAR GLASSES STILL HAVE DIFFICULTY WITH EYESIGHT. (140)**

In winter **13%** of Britons look forward to....summer. **(204)**

**13.9%** of British women do not use a deodorant. **(88)**

**13.6%** of British women own an electric shaver. **(154)**

**13%** of British dwellings are flats or maisonettes. **(139)**

13% of Britons sleep badly most nights. (230)

13% of Britons on the dole openly admit that they do not want to find a job. (239)

13% of British women *never* reach a climax during intercourse itself. (105)

13% of British women under 20 say that they have been rape victims. (105)

13.4% of the British male working population are unemployed. (77)

13% of couples in Yorkshire go to France for their honeymoon. (118)

13% of British women say they date more bisexual men now than they used to. (112)

13% of British people think that scientists, as a breed, are...*style conscious.* (117)

13% of British men who have defective hearing do not wear an aid. (142)

13% of British people prefer 'pants' to 'knickers' as a term of reference for underwear. (150)

13% of British people admit to having problems with literacy and numeracy since leaving school. (36)

# 14%

14% of victims of fatal accidents occurring in British homes are aged 45–64. (136)

14% of British women say that 'tubbiness' turns them off most about the male sex. (245)

14% of British people most like Prince Charles as a member of the Royal Family...and the same amount prefer the Queen Mother. (161)

14% of British boys write love letters...compared to 7% of girls. (176)

14% of British schoolgirls leave school with 2 or more GCE A-levels. (42)

14% of Britons who eat a take-away while watching videos, choose an Indian meal. (205)

14% of Britons are in favour of wheel-clamping. (210)

14% of British women think that David Steel has the nicest personality of all male politicians. (245)

14% of British domestic accidents occur in the garden. (232)

14.5% of the British adult population is defined as Middle Class, Social Grade B. (267)

14% of Britain's Chinese population belong to Social Class AB, Upper Middle Class. (275)

14.8% of the British adult population is defined as Social Grade E, those at the lowest level of subsistence. (267)

14% of British women like looking at pictures of nude men. (104)

14% of Britons go regularly to Church. (111)

14% of British adults suffer *sunburn* in a 12-month period and the same experience bunions, corns, calluses...and constipation. (175)

14% of British 15–25-year-old females feel there is too much violence on television that should not be shown. (12)

14% of Britons believe that men are the safer drivers. (210)

14% of British houses are detached. (139)

**Only** 14% of British women aged 50–59 years got the 'facts of life' from their mothers...and the same percentage learnt in school. (105)

14% of British households have apple pie for pudding at Sunday lunch. (40)

14% of British housewives make suet puddings at home. (20)

14.9% of British males aged 18–44 suffered indigestion in the previous month. (38)

**14% OF BRITISH WOMEN PREFER TO TAKE A PASSIVE ROLE WHEN KISSING. (89)**

14.6% of British housewives who watch TV-am for one hour or more a week own a...fish. (88)

14.9% of British females over 18 years are defined as obese. (38)

14% of British women suffered acute sickness in 1984. (38)

14% of British women say their husbands would like a microwave as a gift. (40)

14% of British families with dependent children are one parent families. (51)

14.7% of British high earners play tennis. (56)

14% of British young women aged 15–34 believe they can catch AIDS from sneezes or tears. (76)

14% of British men ignore any weight gain. (90)

14% of British adults regard Mr Gorbachov unfavourably. (103)

14% of British women make love four times each week. (105)

**14% OF YOUNG BRITONS SUPPORT THE NATIONAL FRONT OR THE BRITISH MOVEMENT. (54)**

14% of British women have changed their bank three times or more. (114)

14% of British people prefer black knickers. (150)

14% of British men say that it is a woman's mouth that most turns them on...10% go for the hips and 4% the hands. (287)

14% of Britons aged 35–50 say that making love is more sexy if there is a chance of pregnancy...66% disagree. (288)

14% of Britons suffer from phobias. (294)

14.3% of British readers of *True Romances*...are men. (88)

# 15%

15% of all readers of women's magazines are...men. (125)

15% of British people think that Labour will win the next General Election. (137)

15% of British people cannot name any member of the Royal Family as their favourite. (163)

15% of the British clergy believe that practising homosexual clergy should be removed from office. (168)

15% of British blood is Rhesus negative. (206)

15% of British men who go in for homosexual activity are married. (105)

15% of British people who regularly drink alcohol, drink whisky in a wine bar. (41)

15% of British men keep a torch in their bedroom. (230)

15% of British women have six to ten orgasms each week. (105)

15% of British men, while making love, fantasize about being watched...or watching others make love. (238)

15% of British men have been to a prostitute. (238)

15% of the British adult population are members of a Christian Church. (17)

15% of British men with sexual problems say they have difficulty getting or maintaining an erection. (238)

15% of British women think that 'Fergie', Duchess of York, has the best head of hair of all female personalities. (245)

15% of British married women say their best friend is their mother. (250)

15% of Britons think that politicians should set better examples in manners. (259)

15% of British single women aged 18–49 cohabit. (263)

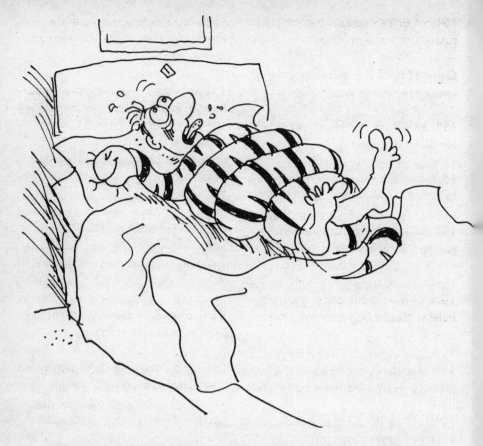

## 15% OF BRITISH PET OWNERS WOULD SOMETIMES, OR ALWAYS, RATHER SLEEP WITH THEIR PET THAN ANYONE ELSE. (74)

**15.8%** of mail delivered in the United Kingdom consists of bills. **(121)**

**15%** of British adults used a wallpaper stripper in the previous 12 months. **(27)**

**15%** of British men like their women to wear G-strings. **(150)**

**15%** of British men played snooker in the four weeks prior to interview. **(38)**

**15%** of British males buy hair conditioner. **(73)**

**15%** of British women describe their bank manager as patronizing. **(114)**

15% of British people cut their toenails in the bath. (230)

**Only** 15% of the British population eat out regularly. (58)

15% of British adults use remedies for diarrhoea. (306)

15.7% of British women have greasy hair. (88)

15% of British married couples had not kissed each other on the lips in the week before interview. (89)

15% of British pet owners do not believe that 'a dog is a man's best friend'. (74)

15% of British women have a body massage when they want to relax. (107)

15% of British young women aged 15–34 believe they can catch AIDS from using the same utensils. (76)

15% of British men use aftershave before going to bed. (90)

15% of British men let their women choose their wardrobe for them. (97)

15% of British women pay the mortgage or rent for the conjugal home. (101)

15% of British women have made love with more than one man during the course of an evening. (105)

15% of British women make love twice each week...and a further 15% do it once. (105)

15% of Britons say that if there were a General Election tomorrow, they would support the Liberal/SDP Alliance. (304)

15% of all British accidental deaths are caused by fires. (232)

15% of British employers perceive a candidate who wears a club-style tie as a reliable member of the establishment. (272)

15% of all Britain's ethnic minority people feel that the police pick on Afro-Caribbeans unfairly. (275)

15% of Britons over 35 years first made love to their partner in a car. (301)

# 16%

16% of British women first made love on the floor. (301)

16% of London taxi drivers suffer from anxiety. (216)

16% of British schoolchildren use their dinner money for gambling. (302)

16% of British women think a beard makes a man look intelligent. (1)

16% of British people think that service in shoe shops is poor. (7)

16% of British 20–25-year-olds believe there will be world peace in their lifetime. (12)

16.7% of British women weigh over 10.5 stone. (107)

16% of British people stay away from the dentist through fear and perceived cost. (57)

16% of British women say they would try making love in a 'threesome', with a man and a woman. (105)

16% of British couples would prefer to have girl babies. (118)

16% of British women never eat red meat. (107)

16% of British high earners (£25,000+ annual household income) smoke. (56)

16% of British people are very dissatisfied with the National Health Service. (35)

16% of British people say they feel confused or dizzy when wearing bifocals. (134)

16% of British men who buy their partner's underwear buy it too big. (150)

16% of the British population speak French. (157)

16% of British men would like to spend Valentine's Day with Selina Scott. (246)

16% of British adults suffer migraine in a 12-month period. (175)

**16%** of British women say that Bruce Willis is their ideal man. **(319)**

**16%** of British women say they have three orgasms each week...and the same percentage have none. **(105)**

**16%** of British men say they buy a new tie because they haven't got a clean one. **(272)**

**Only 16%** of Britons have a cup of tea or coffee when they wake in the morning. **(285)**

**16%** of British DIY consumers are classified as 'Perfectionist Petes'. **(308)**

**16%** of the British population are approached by the police each year in connection with some sort of offence or possible offence. **(120)**

**16%** of British pet owners do not believe it true that Britain is a nation of pet lovers. **(74)**

**16%** of British women keep a torch in their bedroom...and **16%** of British men keep a Bible there. **(230)**

**16%** of British women say that arguments over money are the cause of violence in their marriage. **(319)**

**16%** of Britons are teetotal. **(116)**

**16%** of British women and 25% of men believe in the existence of flying saucers. **(346)**

..... Bot Bots...... Double beds... .... Nylons..... Cross-your-heart bras......

**16% OF BRITISH WOMEN SAY THEY MIGHT TRY 'SAYING NAUGHTY THINGS' TO THEIR PARTNER IN BED. (105)**

# 17%

17% of British people feel that America is a greater threat to world peace than Russia. (35)

17% of the British clergy disagree that Christ was born of a Virgin. (168)

17% of British men shave in their pyjamas. (285)

17% of British women think that a beard on a man makes him good-looking. (1)

17% of British households keep a large dog as a crime prevention measure. (4)

17% of British 15–26-year-old females worry a lot about the risk of getting AIDS. (12)

17% of British women suffer depression. (38)

17% of British adults never use a deodorant or anti-perspirant. (19)

17% of British marriages are between older women and younger men. (70)

17% of British women aged 15–34 believe they can catch AIDS from kissing.(76)

17% of British men ask their wives or girlfriends to account for what they have spent. (86)

17.9% of British women have grey hair. (88)

17% of British men write letters in bed...and 17% of personal letters are posted on Tuesdays. (90 /176)

17% of British women suffer from eczema. (107)

17% of British people think that scientists, as a breed, are...dull. (117)

17% of the British population are aged 45–49. (127)

17% of British women say they experienced their first sexual feelings below the age of 10. (105)

17% of British women prefer a romantic atmosphere when they kiss. (89)

Of the six million accident cases seen by hospital casualty departments each year in Britain, **17%** occur during sporting activities. (136)

**17%** of British men say they buy gold for their women to prove they are worth spending money on. (135)

**17%** of British companies give their staff turkeys for Christmas. (151)

**17%** of British adults avoid caffeine for health reasons. (175)

**17%** of British people take their home holidays in towns and cities. (162)

**17%** of British adults buy take-away food every week. (186)

**17%** of British nurses have been threatened by patients over the last year. (192)

**17%** of British Labour Party members own stocks and shares. (196)

**17%** of British women in the South admit to being secret savers. (203)

**17%** of British men say they do crosswords when they are supposed to be working...and **44%** say they read newspapers, magazines or books. (285)

**17% OF BRITISH ADULTS
SUFFER FROM AN
OILY/GREASY SKIN IN A
12-MONTH PERIOD. (175)**

**17%** of Britons who eat take-away while watching videos, choose fish and chips. **(205)**

**17.3%** of the Scottish population are teetotal. **(116)**

**17%** of British households have more than one car or van. **(51)**

**17%** of British men would like to spend Valentine's Day with Anne Diamond. **(246)**

**17%** of British women have been engaged three times. **(246)**

**17.6%** of the British adult population is defined as Working Class, Social Grade D. **(267)**

**17%** of the British workforce travel to work on public transport. **(285)**

**17%** more British women use antifreeze than their male counterparts. **(204)**

**17%** of British men wear their underwear in bed. **(150)**

**17%** of the British population did not read a single book in 1987. **(233)**

**17%** of British 22–25-year-old men have had more than ten lovers. **(238)**

**Only 17%** of Britain's top businessmen are rated as honest. **(312)**

**17%** of British women say they always have an orgasm during petting or intercourse. **(105)**

**17%** of Britain's ethnic minorities are Muslim. **(275)**

# 18%

18% of British men occasionally go knickerless. (150)

18% of British 15–25-year-old males worry a lot about the risk of getting AIDS. (12)

18% of British adults have read a book about wine. (41)

18% of British women feel that their lover is physically a weed. (48)

18% of British men, while making love to their partner, fantasize about making love to someone else. (238)

18% of British women cry frequently. (107)

18% of British high earners play golf. (56)

18.5% of British men are trying to slim. (88)

Only 18% of British men hang their clothes up after undressing. (90)

18% of British men in the North most want to have breakfast with Samantha Fox. (160)

18% of British couples are surgically sterile. (221)

18% of British women keep ashtrays in their bedroom. (230)

18% of British men put on their slippers before dinner. (230)

18% of British men say they never see erotic literature and films. (238)

18% of British married men having affairs find them less satisfying sexually than their marriage. (238)

18% of British women say that they were sexually abused as children. (105)

18% of British women think Princess Diana is the most stunning woman in the public eye. (245 )

18% of British women think that Joan Collins is the best-dressed of all female personalities. (245)

18% of British women think that Neil Kinnock has the nicest personality of all male politicians. (245)

18% of British men consider cream cakes to be the most romantic food. (246)

18% of British workers in the City say they can identify those working in the field of insurance by their wide and scruffy ties. (272)

18% of British housewives buy morning goods (buns, baps, rolls, croissants, etc.) for afternoon tea. (131)

18% of Britons who have had problems with their telephone service think that BT is not very, or not at all, effective in sorting out the problem. (290)

18% of British men are *fully clothed* when they shave in the morning. (285)

18% of Britons judge standards of honesty among MPs to be high. (312)

18% of British men peek when kissing. (89)

18% of British men have a hangover in a two-week period. (143)

18% of British people most like Princess Anne as a member of the Royal Family. (161)

18% of British people feel that America's power will increase in 1988. (166)

# 19%

19% of British people are *very satisfied* with District Nurses. (35)

19% of British home accidents occur in the kitchen. (232)

19% of British kitchens have fitted carpets. (40)

19% of British men first made love on the floor. (301)

19% of British adults own a portable headphone cassette player. (154)

19% of British women most want to have breakfast with Terry Wogan. (160)

19% of British people would most like to see the Queen if a member of the Royal Family were to come to their area. (163)

**19% OF BRITISH PETS VISIT THE VET TO BE SPAYED OR NEUTERED. (74)**

19% of British adults experienced 'general well-being' in the last two weeks. (175)

19% of homicide victims in England and Wales were strangled. (265)

19% of British households own a cat. (18)

19% of British employers say that they would consider a candidate scruffy if he wasn't wearing a tie. (272)

19% of British *Vogue* readers...are men. (81)

19% of Scottish couples met in pubs. (118)

19% of British men leave the pub before buying their round. (86)

19% of British people think there are people who live in need because of laziness or lack of willpower. (35)

19% of British people say that a married couple on a state pension are really poor. (35)

19% of British men prefer their partner to wear a sexy nightie to make love. (238)

19% of British married men are bothered by premature ejaculation. (238)

19% of British overweight women dream most of wearing tight, revealing clothes once they are slim. (245)

19% of British voters feel that private medicine should be abolished. (249)

19% of British women say that it is a man's chest that most turns them on...14% go for the shoulders. (287)

19% of British DIY consumers are classified as 'Cautious Colins'. (308)

19% of British housewives are ...male. (144)

# 20%

20% of British women, on their first date, ask the man if he has herpes. (112)

20.9% of British readers of *Mother and Baby* magazine are...men. (88)

20% of British candidates have 'virtually no chance of passing their driving test' when they take it. (8)

20% of British households buy flowers every ten days. (345)

20% of British women under 25 years earn between £9,000 and £12,000 per year. (112)

20% of British travellers prefer English 'grub' to 'foreign muck' when on holiday. (14)

20% of British girls are on a diet and the same number eat chocolate most days. (12/107)

20% of British women choose never to have a baby. (93)

20% of British women say they have to make the first move when it comes to love-making. (106)

20% of British women say they prefer men in spectacles. (110)

20% of people in Britain have major psychiatric problems. (69)

20.6% of British adults use artificial sweeteners. (88)

20% of British 17–24-year-olds feel that penalties for drink/driving offences are not severe enough. (94)

20% of Welsh people take, for a hangover cure,...more alcohol. (108)

20% of British women have tried to use feminine charm on their bank manager. (114)

20% of the British population are aged 30–44 years. (128)

20% of the British population are aged 60 or over. (128)

20% of British men most want to have breakfast with Margaret Thatcher. (160)

20% of British women have tried bondage. (105)

20% of the British clergy vote Labour. (168)

20% of British passport owners say that their passport photo makes them look...ugly. (145)

20% of British adults suffer from overeating in a 12-month period. (175)

20% more sons than daughters are born to British butchers. (184)

**More than 20%** of British charitable donations go to Third World countries. (195)

20% of British households have made a major conscious decision to revise their diet as a result of publicity on healthy eating. (40)

20% of British women think their GP prescribes antibiotics too readily. (115)

20% of British men are described as heavy drinkers. (263)

20% of British women say they would never use a vibrator. (105)

20% of British women keep a Bible in their bedroom. (230)

20% of British wives say they *never* turn their husbands down sexually. (238)

20% of British women say they do not think of their partner while making love. (250)

20% of British women make love three times each week. (105)

20% of British women would definitely not tell their husband if they had an affair. (255)

20% of the British population own shares. (263)

20% of the British working population work on Saturdays and Sundays. (17)

20% of Britons still go to work on an egg. (285)

20% of British men say that the first thing they do in the mornings is...dress. (285)

20% of British women say that it is a man's mouth that most turns them on. (287)

20.1% of British women have dry skin. (88)

20% of British men say they would not take any precautions against AIDS if they had a casual affair. (288)

20% of British women say they do not think about sex at all during the day...only 4% of men admit to this.(288)

# 21%

21% of British women use the condom for contraceptive purposes. **(107)**

21% of British men take equal shares with their wives when it comes to looking after the children. **(96)**

21% of British 26–30-year-old men make love with their partner about once a week...21% of 51–60-year-old men make love with their partner *two to three times a week*. **(238)**

21% of British women are single. **(80)**

*No, my husband wasn't at the birth. Why should he be? He wasn't at the conception.*

**21.4% OF ALL LIVE BRITISH BIRTHS ARE ILLEGITIMATE.**
**(262)**

21% of Scottish couples stay in Scotland for their honeymoons. (118)

21% of brides in Ireland are virgins. (118)

21% of London bridegrooms do the washing up. (118)

21% of Britons, in the immediate aftermath of the Chernobyl accident, felt that nuclear power stations create slight, or hardly any, risks for the future. (35)

21% of the British population are under 15 years. (128)

21% of British people most like the Queen as a member of the Royal Family. (161)

21% of Britons make overseas telephone calls on Christmas Day. (207)

21% of the British population said they had never been into a bookshop in 1987. (233)

21% of British women suffer from asthma. (107)

21% of British adults suffer from arthritis/rheumatism in a 12-month period. (175)

21% of British women say that they might try making love in the bath. (105)

21% of British men consider chocolate to be the most romantic food. (246)

21% of all male absence from work is caused by heart and circulatory disorders. (256)

21% of the British working population work on Saturdays. (17)

21.9% of Britons agree that they are workaholics. (307)

21% of British men wake up between 7 and 7.30 a.m. on weekdays. (285)

21% of British adult males have no natural teeth. (42)

21% of British women would prefer to make love to their partners less often. (82)

21% of Welsh men believe that girls who wear glasses are less attractive. (110)

21% of British couples do not talk while making love. (105)

# 22%

**22.6%** of the British adult population is defined as Social Grade C2, Skilled Working Class. **(267)**

**22%** of British women would like to be alone with Paul Newman, undo his tie and unbutton the top of his shirt...half that number would like to do it to Richard Gere. **(272)**

**22%** of British workers have met more than ten spouses of the people they work with. **(285)**

**22%** of British adults use laxatives and salts. **(88)**

**22%** of British men say they never cook. **(230)**

**22% OF BRITISH HOUSEWIVES PURCHASED MULTIVITAMINS IN THE PRECEDING YEAR. (10)**

22% of the British population have a household income of £4,999 or less. (78)

22% of British men wear underwear in bed...but not socks. (90)

22% of British men shave before going to bed. (90)

22% of British women think their men's bodies need attention. (90)

22% of British men care for their complexion. (90)

22% of British teenagers have already had three or four lovers. (105)

22% of British people believe they get the best cup of coffee in France. (109)

22% of the British population are aged 16–29 years. (128)

22% of adult females in England and Wales have never married. (127)

22% of British housewives claim that their husbands never cook, clean, or wash up...whilst only 11% of their husbands claim that this is so. (144)

22% of British adults suffer from sickness/nausea in a 12-month period and the same amount suffer toothache. (175)

22% of British weddings take place at 3 p.m. (211)

22% of British women put on their slippers before dinner. (230)

22% of British husbands who have had affairs say that they have had anywhere from five to more than 20 sexual relationships outside their marriage. (238)

22% of British people aged 16–30 claim that they have never had sex. (250)

22% of British mothers would like to see their daughters choose the Church as a career. (255)

22% of British males over 18 years eat chips on most days. (38)

22% of British 15–25-year-old males feel that a woman's place is in the home. (12)

22% of British households eat breakfast in the sitting-room. (40)

22% of Scottish people who drink alcohol, drink whisky regularly. (41)

22% of British men in the South most want to have breakfast with Selina Scott. (160)

Only 22% of Britons think that the City is honourable. (314)

**22%** of British women most want to have breakfast with Paul Newman. **(160)**

**22%** of British people feel that the escapades of the young Royals have damaged the family's standing. **(163)**

**22%** of British schoolboys leave school with a GCE O-level in Physics. **(42)**

**22%** of British women say they have contemplated *suicide* at least once because of their man's behaviour or lack of concern. **(319)**

**Only 22%** of Britons think that the 'quality press' reporting is accurate. . . and a further **2%** believe the tabloid press. **(318)**

**22%** of all children killed or injured on British roads are pedal cyclists. **(232)**

**22.7%** of the British adult population is defined as Social Grade C1, Lower Middle Class. **(267)**

**22%** of British men who buy their partner's underwear, buy it too small. **(150)**

**22%** of Britain's 'eligible' men choose Felicity Kendall as the celebrity most resembling their ideal woman. **(342)**

**22%** of Britons would support the government selling the Water Authorities. **(323)**

# 23%

23.2% of British housewives use tinned dog food. **(88)**

23% of British women think that a beard on a man makes him look 'experienced'. **(1)**

23% of British manual workforce get five weeks or more annual holiday. **(5)**

23% of British 20–25-year-olds believe that there will be a nuclear war in their lifetime. **(12)**

23% of British 20–25-year-old males feel they might smash things up when angry. **(12)**

23% of British adults have visited a vineyard. **(41)**

**Only 23%** of British women say their partner is their dream lover. **(83)**

23% of British men wear pyjamas or a nightshirt in bed. **(90)**

23% of British women think their men are as bitchy as they are. **(84)**

23% of British people feel that Britain's general industrial performance will decline over the next year. **(35)**

23% of British couples have made love under the influence of marijuana. **(105)**

23% of British homes have security chains fitted. **(113)**

23.7% of British women have dry hair. **(88)**

23% of British people buy jewellery for themselves. **(135)**

23% of British households own a typewriter. **(154)**

23% of British people feel that the Royal Family is less respected nowadays. **(161)**

23% of British adults suffer from acne/pimples/spots in a 12-month period. **(175)**

23% of British letter writers prefer blue writing paper. **(176)**

**23%** of British young men enjoy 'a great deal' the first time they have sexual intercourse. **(238)**

**23%** of British women are not happy with their male partner's attitude to love-making. **(105)**

**23%** of Britons agree strongly that all abortions should be stopped. **(281)**

**23%** of Britons think that gas charges are unreasonable. **(290)**

**23%** of British DIY consumers are classified as 'Dabbler Dannies'...and a further 23% as 'Cheerful Charlies'. **(308)**

**23%** of British couples have tried making love in a swimming pool, a jacuzzi or the sea. **(105)**

**23%** of homicide victims in England and Wales were killed by strangers. **(265)**

## 23% OF BRITISH HOUSEWIVES NEVER BUY FRESH FISH. (26)

# 24%

24% of British homes are owner-occupied, owned outright. (51)

24% of British couples read after going to bed and before falling asleep on Saturday nights. (60)

24% of British men eat in bed. (90)

24.6% of British adults drink British sherries and wines. (88)

24% of British people feel that Prince Edward's decision to quit the Marines was wrong. (161)

24% of British 40–45-year-old women listen to Radio 1. (172)

24% of British adults suffer from stress and anxiety problems in a 12-month period. (175)

24% of British people write letters to pen-friends. (176)

24% of British men keep ashtrays in their bedroom. (230)

24% of British women think that 'Fergie', Duchess of York, has the best-looking body of all female royal personalities. (245)

24% of British women think that David Owen has the best-looking body of all male politicians. (245)

24.3% of British employees work in manufacturing industries. (155)

24% of complaints by British women over harassment in offices concern sexual propositioning....24% of the harassers are immediate supervisors...and a further 24% are members of the management. (316)

24% of white Britons think that ethnic minority children have brought down the standards of education in schools. (275)

24% of Britons aged 35–50 met their present partner at a dance or disco. (288)

24% of British men prefer striped ties...and 24% of London's bankers and stockbrokers believe they can tell how well-off a man is by his tie. (272)

24% of British women are embarrassed by the way their men dress. (97)

24% of British women consider that their men look ridiculous in their underwear *(sic)*. (150)

24% of British men prefer their women to wear camiknickers. (150)

24% of British women spent less than £50 on clothes (outerwear) in the preceding year. (10)

24% of British households own a dog. (18)

24% of British households own a deep-fat fryer. (37)

24% of British couples argue about not helping each other with household chores at weekends. (60)

24% of British wives with full-time jobs are discontent with the lack of domestic help from their partners. (273)

24% of British husbands claim that they do a large food shop once a week or more often whilst *only 18%* of their wives claim this is so. (144)

24% of Britain's 'eligible' young men say they see their ideal woman driving a racy and fast car. (342)

24% of Britons think of poverty and decay when they hear the term 'inner cities'. (320)

24% of British husbands having affairs cite a poor sexual relationship with their wife as the reason. (238)

24% of British women use depilatories. (88)

24% of British householders take no steps to improve security in their homes. (113)

24% of Scottish couples would prefer to have girl babies. (118)

24% of the Chinese population of Great Britain were born in the UK. (127)

24% of British people kiss their parents on the lips. (89)

24% of British teenagers have a hangover in a two-week period. (143)

24% of British adolescent boys have had sexual intercourse for the first time under the age of 16. (238)

# 25%

25% of British women aged 15–34 claim to be virgins. (76)

25% of bridegrooms in Ireland are virgins on their wedding day. (118)

25% of British women under 18 say they date more bisexual men now than they used to. (112)

25% of British 20–25-year-olds believe there will be a 'United States' of Europe in their lifetime. (12)

25% of British meals are boiled or steamed. (37)

25% of British adults have no teeth. (57)

25% of Britons sing in the bath. (230)

25% of Britons do not bother to lock the bathroom door. (286)

25% of British pets sleep in the kitchen. (74)

25% of British people feel that Britain's general industrial performance will improve over the next year. (35)

25% of British men would feel threatened if their partner earned more than them. (112)

25% of British women would like their men to be taller. (83)

25% of British men are put off kissing women who wear too much lipstick. (89)

25% of British families cook their Sunday roast in a microwave. (111)

25% of British people believe they get the best cup of coffee in Britain. (109)

25% of British women have a female GP. (115)

25% of British people feel there are people who live in need because of injustice in our society. (35)

25% of British people feel that sharing chores is very important to a successful marriage. (35)

25% of British housholds contain only one person. **(263)**

25% of British households own heated hair rollers. **(10)**

25% of British men say they talk to their wives during breakfast...only 16% of women talk to their husbands. **(285)**

25% of Britons manage to get up in the mornings and out of the house in less than 30 minutes. **(285)**

25% of British men say that the major topic of conversation at work is...sport. **(285)**

25% of Britons watch 'Neighbours' on television Monday to Friday. **(296)**

25.5% of British adults suffered from flu in the last 12 months. **(88)**

**Around 25%** of health districts in England and Wales have no doctors able to cope with heart attacks or fit pacemakers. **(310)**

Mum, Dad, I'm getting married

**25% OF BRITISH MEN HAVE DRESSED UP AS A WOMAN AT SOME TIME. (238)**

25% of British women occasionally go knickerless. (150)

25% of British women go to bed between 10.31 and 11.00 p.m. (285)

25% of British people think that thermal underwear is *fashionable*. (150)

25% of British people over 55 years believe that 'writing letters is old-fashioned'. (176)

25% of Britons believe that women are the safer drivers. (210)

25% of British men say that they used to feel guilty about sex. (238)

25% of British men say that their partners mind when they look at pornographic material. (238)

25% of British men who have had affairs admit that it worsened the emotional relationship between them and their wives. (238)

25% of British fathers say that they find it difficult to relate to their children. (238)

25% of British men who consider themselves bisexual are currently having homosexual relationships. (238)

25% of British women suffering premenstrual syndrome describe themselves as *violent* at this time of the month. (149)

25% of British women report that they have had seven or more lovers. (105)

25% of British mothers would like their daughters to choose 'manual work' as a career. (255)

**Only 25%** of British 16-year-olds attempt GCE O-levels. (269)

25% of Britons who live in inner cities would prefer to live in the countryside. (320)

# 26%

**26%** of British men would wear *socks with sandals*. **(97)**

**26%** of British men allow pets to snuggle up in their beds. **(39)**

**26%** of British mothers would like their daughters to join the fire brigade as a career. **(255)**

**26%** of British women think their waists are their best feature. **(107)**

**26%** of British men, when they go to bed later than their partners, will wake them to say goodnight. **(90)**

**26%** of British people consider the cost of heating and lighting to be the most worrying aspects of daily life. **(113)**

**26%** of British householders would like to fit a burglar alarm. **(113)**

**26%** of children who were adopted in England and Wales in 1984 were aged ten years or over. **(17)**

**26.9%** of British men do not use a deodorant. **(88)**

**26%** of British adults suffer from sleeping problems in a 12-month period. **(175)**

**26%** of British people took no holiday at all in the last five years. **(162)**

**26%** of British chief executives are under 40. **(197)**

**26%** of British men are not happy with the frequency of their partner's orgasms. **(238)**

**26%** of British women say they never experience simultaneous orgasms with their partner. **(105)**

**26%** of British husbands admit to having a sexual relationship outside their marriage. **(238)**

**26%** of British people believe that the creation of a merged Alliance party from the old SDP and Liberal parties would make them less likely to vote for it. **(241)**

**26%** of British men aged 75 and over live alone. **(263)**

26% of British people like David Steel and his policies. 26% don't. (137)

26% of British men think David Steel was the smartest tie-wearer during the General Election. (272)

26.3% of Britons disapprove of aerosol cans because of the effect on the atmosphere. (307)

26% of British people own Premium Bonds. (138)

26% of British people would prefer to spend Christmas Day in a hotel. (135)

26.7% of British women have a tendency to dandruff. (88)

26% of British people feel that the Royal Family is more respected nowadays. (161)

26% of British people feel that 1988 will be a peaceful year, more or less free of international disputes... (166)

26% of the British clergy vote Conservative. (168)

26% of British adults have never seen a doctor for a general check-up. (175)

Well, I'm telling you the computer made an error. I only ordered one beef Vindaloo

**26% OF BRITISH ADULTS LIKE THE IDEA OF SHOPPING BY HOME COMPUTER. (30)**

# 27%

27% of British household accidental fires are first ignited with cooking fat. (136)

Only 27% of Northern men dare to shop alone when buying presents for their partners. (135)

27% of British companies give their staff free days' holiday at Christmas. (151)

27.1% of British households own a home computer. (154)

27% of British 40–54-year-old women spend between £150 and £400 a year on cosmetics. (172)

27% of British MPs say that they have received a letter which has been instrumental in changing Government policy. (177)

27% of British husbands say their wives understand them completely. (238)

27% of British husbands say that kissing and cuddling is more important to their wives than intercourse. (238)

27% of British adults have never stayed in an English, Welsh or Scottish hotel for pleasure. (21)

27% of British women think their men have a flair for fashion. (97)

27% of British adults consider 'British make' to be the most important factor when buying a bicycle. (22)

27% of British housewives watch breakfast television at least once a week while having breakfast. (40)

27% of the British population who read the *Financial Times*...are women. (78)

27% of British people feel that Education should be the highest priority for extra government spending. (35)

27% of British Conservatives feel that poverty will increase over the next ten years. (35)

27% of British Labour supporters feel there is very little real poverty in Britain. (35)

27% of British women say that reports of sex diseases have recently made them alter their own sexual behaviour. (105)

27% of British overweight women dream most of wearing jeans once they are slim. (245)

27% of British mothers would like their sons to choose the Church as a career. (255)

27% of British wives work full-time. (263)

27% of British infant deaths are caused by congenital anomalies. (232)

**Shotguns are used in 27.4%** of robbery offences involving firearms in England and Wales. (265)

27% of Britons believe that racial discrimination in this country is a very serious problem. (295)

27% of Britain's ethnic minority people believe in repatriation...21% of white Britons believe this would help solve racial problems. (295)

27% of Britons would support the government selling The Post Office. (323)

**Only 27%** of British married men put any emphasis on their own fidelity. (238)

27% of British people think that scientists as a breed are eccentric. (117)

27.1% of British adults buy car shampoo. (88)

27% of British men help their women with their coats. (319)

**27% OF LONDON'S BANKERS AND STOCKBROKERS SAY THAT A MAN'S CHOICE OF TIE INDICATES HIS AGE. (272)**

# 28%

28% of British 15–25-year-old females feel they might travel on public transport without paying. (12)

28% of British housewives with families say they eat breakfast together. (37)

28% of Britons wear their night clothes or dressing-gown when they have breakfast. (160)

28% of British women think their legs are their best feature. (107)

28% of British customers feel that the job of a hairdresser is one of the best. (7)

28.3% of British adults buy car polish. (88)

28.1% of British high earners own more than two cars. (56)

28% of British adults describe their weekends as 'expensive'. (60)

Only 28% of British people feel that they benefit from pain-relieving prescription drugs. (147)

28.6% of British women are mainly responsible for the upkeep of the garden. (154)

28% of London tube drivers agree that they have too much responsibility at work. (171)

28% of British people think their own standard of living will rise in 1988. (209)

28% of British men say they believe prostitutes provide particular types of sex that men cannot get in their relationships. (238)

28% of British women say that the major topic of conversation at work is their family. (285)

28% of Britons think that water charges are unreasonable. (290)

28.1% of British adults are trying to slim. (88)

28.7% of British consumers felt that business conditions were 'bad' after the stock market collapse in October 1987. (130)

**28%** of British people feel that Britain should disarm unilaterally. **(35)**

**28.5%** of British consumers felt that business conditions were 'good' despite the stock market collapse in October 1987. **(130)**

**28%** of British men feel that the most romantic gift for a woman would be a dozen red roses . . . whilst 43% of women feel that a diamond ring is the most romantic. **(135)**

**28%** of British women wear their underwear in bed. **(150)**

**28%** of British women describe their men as 'thrifty'. **(86)**

**28%** of men in Scotland willingly take turns to clean the lavatory. **(96)**

**28%** of British viewers vote Terry Wogan the best chat-show host. **(119)**

**28%** of British men do not use after-shave lotion. **(88)**

**28% OF BRITISH MEN CONSIDER BEER OR LAGER THE *MOST ROMANTIC* DRINK. (246)**

# 29%

29% of British women count shopping among their most pleasurable leisure activities. (30)

29% of British men aged 16–19 years smoke cigarettes. (15)

29% of British males reported themselves chronically sick in 1985. (38)

29% of British 15–25-year-olds agree with the idea that unemployed people could get a job if they tried. (12)

29% of British women have not seen their men cry. (99)

29% of British people feel that American nuclear missiles make Britain a safer place. (35)

29% of British adults think of themselves as having moved into a higher social class compared with their parents. (127)

29% of English and Welsh schoolchildren rely on packed lunches for their midday meal. (199)

29% of British divorced men say they have seriously regretted parting from their wife at least sometimes. (238)

29% of British women rate their love lives as poor, awful or non-existent. (105)

29.4% of the British population live on council estates. (268)

29% of British housewives wish their husbands would clean the oven. (273)

29% of white Britons feel that television and radio are responsible for trouble between ethnic minorities and the police . . . 26% blame the newspapers. (275)

29% of British women say they never turn to their husbands when they have a problem...27% of them say that he isn't sympathetic enough. (319)

29% of British 'high risk' drivers believe they can drive *more safely* after drinking than before. (208)

**29%** of British bridegrooms proposed to their fiancées six months or less after meeting them. **(211)**

**29.9%** of British women have dark-brown hair. **(88)**

**Only 29%** of Britons taking villa holidays in Spain drink the local tap water. **(322)**

**29%** of British people like Neil Kinnock and his policies. **(137)**

**29.8%** of British adults grow fruit. **(154)**

**29.6%** of British adults grow vegetables. **(154)**

**29.4%** of British households own a fixed car radio. **(154)**

**29%** of British people watch 'Blind Date'. **(129)**

**29%** of British adult males in England and Wales have never married. **(127)**

**29% OF BRITISH PEOPLE DO NOT GO OUT ALONE AFTER DARK. (4)**

# 30%

30% of British people watch 'Coronation Street' on Mondays. (129)

30% of British people watch 'Coronation Street' on Wednesdays. (129)

30% of condoms in Britain are sold to . . . women. (146)

30% of British people opt for plain white when choosing underwear. (150)

30% of British men kill spiders in the bath. (99)

30% of British women belong to a health or sports club. (107)

30% of British adults suffer from flu or a virus in a 12-month period and the same amount experience premenstrual problems. (175)

30% of British men's affairs last from one year to over a decade. (238)

30% of British women say they experience high levels of stress. (254)

30% of Britons never visit the dry-cleaner. (264)

30% of British men say they think about sex often during the day . . . only 5% of women admit this. (288)

30% of British men prefer their women to be monogamous. (112)

30% of British women use no contraception. (107)

30% of British women in Scotland think their man is a weakling. (48)

30% of British women in Wales think their men could outbitch them. (84)

30% of British adult females have no natural teeth. (42)

30% of British wives hide the true cost of Christmas spending from their husbands. (50)

Over 30% of young Britons support a political party of the extreme right. (54)

**30% OF BRITISH WOMEN HAVE TRIED BOTTOM SMACKING
AS A SEXUAL PRACTICE. (105)**

**30%** of Britons agree that any attempt to solve the Northern Ireland problem must have the cooperation of the IRA. **(55)**

**30%** of British women think their men are totally honest. **(87)**

**30%** of British men prefer their women not to be virgins. **(112)**

**30%** of British high earners (£25,000+ annual household income) have three or more cars. **(56)**

**30.6%** of British women have light-brown hair. **(88)**

**30%** of British adults use remedies for rheumatism. **(88)**

**30.5%** of British adults buy chewing gum. **(88)**

**30.1%** of British adults use mouthwashes and gargles. **(88)**

**30%** of British men often have dirty fingernails. **(90)**

**30%** of Britain's 'eligible' men say that the celebrity least resembling their ideal woman is Joan Collins. **(342)**

**30%** of British men use bubblebath. **(90)**

**30%** of British people believe that AIDS can be contracted through being bitten. **(91)**

**30%** of British men dislike getting pyjamas for Christmas. **(50)**

**30%** of British drownings are linked to alcohol. **(187)**

**30%** of British letter writers prefer to use coloured or patterned writing paper. **(176)**

**30%** of British motorists are in favour of automatic prison sentences on convictions of drink-driving offences. **(208)**

# 31%

31% of British people think that Russia would cheat on an arms control agreement. (16)

31% of British women reported themselves chronically sick in 1985. (38)

31% of British overweight women say that chocolate is to blame for their surplus weight. (245)

31% of British men put their dirty washing in the laundry basket. (106)

31% of British people use wholemeal bread to make toast. (40)

31% of British adults regard Ronald Reagan favourably. (103)

31% of British women suffer from anaemia. (107)

31% of British brides would prefer to stay at home rather than work. (118)

31% of British houses are semi-detached. 31% are terraced. (139)

31% of British adults smoke cigarettes. (175)

31% of couples in England and Wales marrying for the first time prefer to use a Registry Office. (202)

31% of British over-65-year-olds prefer to take hot bubble baths together. (204)

31% of British young men do not enjoy the first time they have sexual intercourse. (238)

31% of British households own electric curling tongs. (10)

31% of British men use their personal contacts to help them get jobs. (258)

31% of British deaths of 30–39-year-olds are caused by cancer. (232)

31% of British men choose silk as their favourite material for a tie. (272)

31% of British women agree that night time is the favourite time to make love. (301)

# 32%

Only **32%** of British crimes were solved in 1986. **(263)**

**32%** of homicide victims in England and Wales were killed by a member of their own family. **(265)**

**32%** of British men change into work clothes when they arrive at work . . . 28% of women do so. **(285)**

**32%** of British women say that the size of a partner's organ is important to them. **(105)**

**32%** of British wives work part-time. **(263)**

**32.6%** of British women say that they like to keep up with the latest fashions. **(307)**

**32% OF BRITISH MEN OBJECT TO THEIR PARTNERS GOING TOPLESS ON THE BEACH. (85)**

**32%** of British 15–25-year-old males feel that sex outside marriage is wrong. (12)

**32%** of British 15–25-year-old females feel that they might evade paying tax. (12)

**32%** of British women smoke. (263)

**32%** of British women would like their men to be more exciting. (83)

**Only 32%** of British women are ever suspicious of their men. (87)

**32%** of British adults avoid salt in food for health reasons. (175)

**32%** of British men leave their clothes on the floor after undressing. (90)

**32%** of British men raised as Catholics say they felt guilty about sex. (238)

**32%** of British nurses say they would vote Conservative if there were a general election tomorrow. (344)

**32%** of Britons sleep in the nude in summer. (230)

**32%** of British couples would prefer to have boy babies. (118)

**32%** of British people like Mrs Thatcher and her policies. (137)

**32%** of British people believe the Queen should reign until her death. (161)

**32%** of British teachers say that they have been physically attacked by a pupil. (169)

**32%** of British pregnancies begin outside marriage. (180)

**32%** of British 'high risk' drivers – those who repeatedly drive while being 'over the limit' – believe that they can drink four or more glasses of wine without it affecting their driving. (208)

**32%** of Britons think that crime is the biggest problem facing the inner cities of Britain today. (320)

# 33%

33% of British teenagers have five drinks or more during the week. (2)

33% of the British Indian population were born in the UK. (51)

33% of British households contain two persons. (51)

33% of British people confess to giving old, unwanted presents at Christmas and taking cheap plonk to parties before drinking all the spirits. (50)

Only 33% of British couples survive Christmas without a blazing row. (50)

33% of British women over 20 say they are worried about cervical cancer. (76)

33% of British women aged 15–34 think AIDS can be passed on via saliva. (76)

33% of British women do not like beards . . . on men. (89)

33% of British women think their men are in excellent shape. (90)

Only 33% of British women learnt the 'facts of life' from their mother. (105)

33% of British men who would like to change the way they make love want to be more experimental. (238)

33% of British husbands who have ever been unfaithful are having affairs now. (238)

33% of British women say they cannot reach multiple orgasms. (105)

33% of British women think that Princess Diana has the most attractive face of all female royal personalities. (245)

33% of British men consider a waterbed to be the most romantic honeymoon bed. (246)

33% of British women say they have no friends from other ethnic groups. (255)

33% of British women would not like their child to marry someone of a lower social class. (255)

**33%** of British women, if given the chance to strangle a man with his own tie, would choose to do it to Arthur Scargill . . . Ronald Reagan took 12% of this vote and Neil Kinnock and Tony Blackburn each polled 10%. **(272)**

**33%** of British couples say that one partner manages all the money and gives the other his/her share. **(35)**

**33%** of British adults suffer from stiffness in the joints in a 12-month period. **(175)**

*Answer.. yes, does suffer violent rages*

**33% OF BRITISH TEENAGERS SAY THEY HAVE VIOLENT RAGES. (2)**

**33.8%** of British adults buy antifreeze. **(88)**

**33%** of British consumers still expect their incomes to increase after the stock market collapse in October 1987. **(130)**

**33%** of British men who buy their partner's underwear, choose 'pretty' rather than 'sexy' outfits. **(150)**

**Over 33%** of London cabbies have serious phobias . . . . **(216)**

**33%** of British couples could probably benefit from some form of marriage guidance. **(222)**

**33%** of British pub customers would like to see parts of the bar restricted to non-smokers. **(226)**

**33%** of British women say they would suspect the man in their life was having an affair if he started to dress more smartly. **(333)**

**33%** of Britons watch television for five hours a day or more. **(325)**

**33%** of British men say that the *worst* moments in an ordinary day involve getting up in the morning . . . 28% of women agree. **(285)**

**33%** of British men have to wear a suit where they work. **(285)**

**33%** of Britons agree that racial problems arise in Britain because the police force is racist . . . 47% disagree. **(300)**

**33%** of British single mothers with dependent children cohabit. **(263)**

**33%** of British adults think that local government is well run. **(227)**

**33%** of British pet dogs are bought special Christmas dinners . . .**(50)**

**33%** of Britons, when it comes to insider dealing, say they are quite happy to break the law. **(325)**

**33%** of Britons would support the government selling British Rail. **(323)**

# 34%

34% of British men bitch about someone else's looks. **(84)**

34% of British women allow pets to snuggle up in their beds. **(39)**

34% of British schoolboys in England and Wales have a GCE O-level at grades A – C in English on leaving school. **(42)**

34% of British men claim to do some cooking every day. **(230)**

34% of British adults suffer from indigestion/heartburn in a 12-month period. **(175)**

34% of British men pay all the household bills in the conjugal home. **(101)**

34% of Britons prefer to take black coffee for a hangover cure. **(108)**

34% of British people dislike Neil Kinnock. **(137)**

34% of the British population say they did not go to a public library in 1987. **(233)**

34% of British men say they have no difficulties with reaching a climax. **(238)**

34% of British husbands wish their wives would talk more about how it feels while making love. **(238)**

34% of British women think that 'Fergie', Duchess of York, has the most attractive face of all female royal personalities. **(245)**

34% of British mothers would like to see their daughters choose the armed forces as a career. **(255)**

34% of Britain's ethnic minority people consider their overall housing conditions as bad or very bad. **(275)**

34% of British teenagers feel that Britain should continue to help the Third World even if our standard of living stops improving. **(167)**

34% of British people kiss their children on the lips. **(89)**

34% of British adults who own gardens buy weedkillers. **(154)**

**34%** of the British clergy vote for the Alliance. **(168)**

**34%** of Britons who do not own a telephone *never write letters.* **(176)**

**34%** of British customers feel they often get better service from a machine than a person. **(7)**

**34%** of British men are in favour of the death sentence for the punishment of convicted rapists . . . and 34% of British women agree. **(231)**

**34.2%** of British adults own a portable radio/cassette recorder. **(154)**

**34% OF BRITISH MEN HAVE WORRIED THAT THEIR PENIS WAS TOO SMALL...AND 10% STILL WORRY. (238)**

# 35%

35% of Britons feel that bankers and business journalists are the most trustworthy source for financial advice. (312)

35% of British female fatalities are defined as premature. (38)

35% of British girls aged 17 regularly drink in pubs. (49)

35.6% of British males over 18 years are defined as overweight. (38)

35.3% of Britons like to take holidays in Britain rather than abroad. (307)

35% of British housewives like to meditate. (107)

35% of British adults wear dentures. (88)

35.1% of British women buy stockings. (88)

35.8% of British housewives use ground coffee or coffee bags. (88)

Only 35% of British people who wear glasses keep a second pair for emergencies. (110)

35% of British men, when they are in company, refer to their women with respect and admiration. (112)

35% of British people consider road safety and the fear of losing their jobs to be the most worrying aspects of daily life. (113)

35% of British single clergy approve of homosexuality. (168)

35% of British men keep a television in their bedroom. (230)

35% of Britons have nightmares. (230)

Only 35% of British men feel no need for improvement in their sex life. (238)

35% of Britons think that Neil Kinnock is proving a good leader of the Labour Party. (304)

35% of Britons think that electricity charges are unreasonable. (290)

# 36%

36% of British households own a microwave. (24)

36% of British housewives with families say they eat every meal together. (37)

36% of British men would rather go hungry than cook for themselves. (106)

36% of British wine drinkers never pay more than £3 a bottle for home drinking. (41)

36% of British women think their breasts are their best feature. (107)

36% of British people feel that the standard of service in Great Britain is worse than other countries. (7)

36% of British households have video recorders. (53)

36% of British men take their socks off last when they undress. (90)

Only 36% of British men have ever set a seduction scene in the bedroom. (90)

36% of British men would rather risk a parking ticket than hunt for a space. (106)

36% of British brides say they realize their marriage may not last for ever. (118)

36% of unmarried Britons feel that divorce should be made more difficult to obtain. (35)

36% of new adult residents in the United Kingdom in 1985 are classified as professional and managerial. (127)

36% of British adults own a fountain pen. (176)

36% of British people prefer coloured knickers . . . as opposed to black or white. (150)

36% of British people think that America's power will decline in 1988. (166)

36% of the British clergy are opposed to the ordination of women. (168)

**36%** of British couples say they never argue over money. (101)

**36%** of Britons prefer aluminium foil to plastic film for wrapping food. (199)

**36%** of British people think that the value of the pound against the dollar will rise during 1988. (209)

**36%** of British adolescents say they would obey the law without exception. (227)

**36.9%** of Britons say they really enjoy a night out at the pub. (307)

**36%** of British husbands would like their wives to be more responsive when making love. (238)

**36%** of British men say that the pornographic material they see is a mixture of hard and soft. (238)

**36%** of British men smoke. (263)

**36.8%** of British adults buy car tyres. (88)

**36.7%** of Britons agree that if they had an adequate private income they would never go out to work again. (307)

# 37%

37% of British men fantasize while they make love. **(238)**

37% of British women admit they have caught their men out in a lie. **(87)**

37% of British households are owner-occupied with a mortgage. **(51)**

37% of British men object to their wives wearing revealing clothes. **(85)**

Hand over the carrier bags!

SUPA-STORE

**37% OF BRITISH CUSTOMERS FEEL THEY SHOULD NOT PAY FOR CARRIER BAGS. (7)**

**37%** of Britons say that if there were a General Election tomorrow, they would support the Labour Party. (304)

**37%** of British couples say they are more in love now than on their wedding day. (105)

**37%** of British people feel it an inevitable part of modern life that people live in need. (35)

**37%** of British households have a sandwich maker. (37)

**37%** of British companies give their staff a pay bonus at Christmas. (151)

**37%** of women released from prison in England and Wales are reconvicted within two years. (282)

**37%** of Britons eat over 11 ounces of white, large, wrapped bread per week. (289)

**37%** of British people feel that the Royal Family should not be free to say whatever they like to the Press. (163)

**37%** of British people believe that taxes will fall in 1988. (166)

**37%** of British women are trying to slim. (88)

**37%** of British pregnancies that begin outside marriage end in abortion. (180)

**37%** of British marriages in England and Wales are remarriages. (202)

**37%** of Britons watch rented videos on Saturdays. (205)

**37%** of Britons never invite friends in for a drink. (230)

**37%** of British husbands who have never had an affair either wish they had or feel tempted. (238)

**37.2%** of Britons say they would prefer to buy British but the quality is not good enough. (307)

# 38%

38% of British 20–25-year-olds believe there will be an increase in communism in their lifetime. (12)

38% of British people think that America would cheat on an arms control agreement. (16)

38.5% of British women aged 18–44 suffered from a headache during the previous month. (38)

38% of British couples make love three to five times a week. (82)

38% of British women who are hit by their men stand by them. (319)

38% of British women suffer from allergies. (107)

38% of British men, when they cut their finger, rush to their woman's arms. (99)

38% of British people do not drink wine. (41)

38.2% of British people drink shandy. (88)

38% of Britons know of people who have claimed insurance compensation for totally invented losses . . . the most popular invention is the expensive camera supposedly dropped overboard while on holiday. (235)

38% of British men say that their partner refuses their requests to try something different sexually . . . only 3% of men refuse their partner's request to try a new position or technique. (238)

Only 38% of British married men who have had affairs say that they were more satisfying sexually than their marital relationship. (238)

38% of British women think that Princess Diana has the best-looking body of all the female royal personalities. (245)

38% of British young women own designer clothes. (252)

38% of homicide victims in England and Wales were killed with a 'sharp instrument'. (265)

**38%** of British people consider Education to be the most worrying aspect of daily life. **(113)**

**38.1%** of British adults who own gardens buy fertilizers. **(154)**

**38.3%** of British women own a sewing machine. **(154)**

**38%** of Britons buy their stockings from grocers. **(183)**

**38%** of Britons are in favour of the introduction of condom machines in schools. **(182)**

**38%** of British 15–25-year-old females feel that sex outside marriage is wrong. **(12)**

**38%** of Britons under 24 say they make love with their present partner after a month of going out with them. **(287)**

**38%** of British children say that their fathers swear while driving. **(305)**

**38% OF BRITISH MEN OWN A BOW TIE...29% OF THESE ARE LIKELY TO WORK IN ADVERTISING. (272)**

# 39%

39% of British men never make a proper meal. **(96)**

39% of British mothers buy their children's clothes at Marks & Spencer. **(23)**

39% of British women say they don't get affection from their partners after making love. **(82)**

39% of British women in Wales say they would not choose their current partner if they could make love just once more in their life. **(82)**

39% of Britons feel that the most urgent problem facing the country is the Health Service. **(304)**

39% of British people breakfast alone. **(160)**

39% of London tube drivers say they return home over-tired . . . and 39% say they do not. **(171)**

39% of British couples have tried making love in exotic places – on beaches, in cars, in trains, in aeroplanes, in *lavatories*. **(105)**

39% of Britons wish Britain to leave the European Community. **(190)**

39% of British men sometimes climax too quickly. **(238)**

39% of British husbands had had no previous lovers before they met their wife. **(238)**

39% of British single women say that they have committed adultery. **(105)**

39% of Britain's Chinese population speak mainly English at home. **(275)**

39% of Britain's ethnic minority people agree that most of them don't have a good enough education to get good jobs. **(275)**

# 40%

40% of British teenagers eat white bread every day. (12)

40% of British women think that pubs should stay open longer in the afternoons. (6)

40% of the British workforce are women. (38)

40% of British women dislike ironing. (40)

40% of British consumers vote 'queues' one of the most common causes for complaint. (7)

40% of probation officers in England and Wales are female. (120)

40% of British people say they might try making love in front of a video camera . . . while it is turned on. (105)

40% of Britons favour some sort of withdrawal strategy with regard to British troops in Northern Ireland. (55)

40% of British men say they have regular dental check-ups. (42)

40% of British women take regular exercise. (107)

40% of British men cast aspersions on the IQs of others. (84)

40% of British women say their men regard them as equals. (112)

40% of British households have a mail-order catalogue. (72)

40% of British cat owners *believe their pet knows it's Christmas*. (50)

40% of the drinkers in Wales admit to over-indulgence. (108)

40% of British men feel threatened by their partner's women friends. (112)

40% of British adults approach the police each year for matters unrelated to crime. (120)

40% of British women have actually met their bank manager. (114)

40% of the total non-white population is UK-born. (266)

40% of British people watch 'EastEnders' on Tuesdays and Sundays. (129)

40% of British people watch 'EastEnders' on Thursdays and Sundays. (129)

40% of all fatal accidents in the United Kingdom occur in the home. (136)

40.8% of British women prefer their men to wear boxer shorts to briefs. (150)

40% of British people feel that Prince Harry and Prince William should have a spell in state education. (161)

40% of British people think that 1988 will be a troubled year with much worldwide discord. (166)

40% of British 17-year-olds feel that gays should be prosecuted. (2)

40% of British holidaymakers now venture out of their hotels to eat out in restaurants. (200)

40% of British women have used a vibrator. (105)

40% of the British working-classes would refuse a driver a drink . . . only 19% of the upper classes would do this. (208)

Over 40% of Britain's gifted children show signs of under-achievement in state schools. (219)

40% of British adults think that the Civil Service is well run. (227)

40% of British heterosexual couples practise rectal intercourse. (105)

40% of Britons sing to themselves every day. (230)

40% of British men who want to make changes in the way they make love want to be more skilful. (238)

40% of British men who have no children or whose children have left home say that they are very happy with their sex life. (238)

40% of British women did not use any form of contraception the first time they had sexual intercourse. (105)

40% of British women say they have tried applying wine, cream and other tasty items to parts of the body as part of love play. (105)

40.2% of British adults drink cider. (88)

40% of British women say that they would not be happy for their child to marry someone of a different race. (255)

# 41%

41% of British 15–25-year-old females worry a lot about being attacked at night. (12)

41.8% of British women prefer their men to wear briefs rather than boxer shorts. (150)

41% of British men in England and Wales aged 65 will survive to reach 80 years. (38)

41% of British 15–25-year-old males believe that women should fight for total equality. (12)

41% of British people say they know hardly anything about wine. (41)

41% of British women think their men like to present a macho image of themselves to the world. (99)

41.5% of British men are mainly responsible for the upkeep of their gardens. (154)

41% of British women would most like to spend Valentine's Day with Gary 'Bit in the Middle' Davies. (246)

41% of British mothers would like their sons and daughters to choose politics as a career . . . and 41% of mothers would like their daughters to join the police. (255)

41% of British women use their personal contacts to help them get jobs. (258)

41% of British women have a driving licence. (263)

41% of British men are woken by an alarm on weekday mornings. (285)

41% of British men say that seeing someone attractive makes them think of sex . . . 41% of women start thinking about sex when they think of their lover. (288)

41.4% of Britons think that a lot of advertising patronizes women. (307)

41.9% of Britons think they have a good sense of style. (307)

41% of Britons never invite friends in for a formal meal. (230)

**41%** of British mothers with young children put 'things' in the kitchen bin between 6 and 20 times a day. **(273)**

**41.2%** of British adults own a portable radio. **(154)**

**41% OF BRITISH HUSBANDS ADMIT TO BUYING LINGERIE FOR THEIR LOVED ONES AT CHRISTMAS EVEN THOUGH THEY FIND IT A *TOTALLY EMBARRASSING EXPERIENCE.* (50)**

# 42%

42% of British men seldom ask their women what pleases them sexually. (112)

42% of Britons feel that many people would eat healthier food if the rest of their families would let them. (35)

42.4% of British women prefer their sexy lingerie to be white. (150)

42% of British people think that the NHS represents value for money to the taxpayer. (132)

42% of British people who consult alternative medicine practitioners find the treatments completely successful and free from adverse side-effects. (147)

42.5% of British women suffering premenstrual syndrome say they go out of their way to pick a quarrel at this time of the month. (149)

42% of Britons think that judges should be able to give the death sentence in the case of all murders. (231)

42% of British married men with sexual difficulties say that the problem is their wife's lack of interest in sex. (238)

42% of small businesses in Britain are started up by female entrepreneurs. (32)

42% of Britons feel that stockbrokers are the most trustworthy source for financial advice. (312)

42% of British men prefer plain neckties . . . and 42% of City workers consider Old School ties to be the most suitable type for stockbrokers. (272)

42% of the British adult population had some cause to complain about goods and services over the last 12 months. (292)

42% of Britons approve of the government's record to date. (304)

42.2% of British adults use indigestion and stomach remedies. (88)

**42% OF BRITISH CATS ARE KILLED IN ROAD ACCIDENTS.**
**(188)**

42% of British high earners work in the private sector. **(56)**

42% of British women aged 15–34 would 'reluctantly' accept an internal examination. **(76)**

42% of men in Scotland wear *socks with sandals*. **(97)**

42% of British men who have problems in their sex lives and children under five say that their problems are connected with pregnancy and/or childbirth. **(238)**

42.4% of British adults suffered a 'stuffy nose' in the last 12 months. **(88)**

# 43%

43% of British people feel that the Government should redistribute income from the better-off to those who are less well-off. (35)

43% of British people feel that the Royal Family should not accept valuable gifts. (161)

43% of British teenagers feel that the Third World is exploited by developed countries. (167)

43% of British motorists are in favour of lowering the alcohol limit. (208)

43% of English blood belongs to Group A. (206)

43% of British men say that the first time they had intercourse it was out of pure curiosity. (238)

43% of British men prefer their partner to wear stockings and suspenders to make love. (238)

43% of British women say they masturbate as part of love-play with their husbands. (105)

43% of British men prefer blue ties. (272)

43% of British bridegrooms wear morning dress to their weddings. (293)

43% of Britons say they disapprove of the law allowing homosexual relations between consenting adults in private. (315)

43% of British mothers would like their sons to choose nursing as a career. (255)

43% of British men never clean the lavatory. (96)

43% of British housewives feel guilty over the amount of domestic rubbish thrown away. (273)

43% of British people think that the Royal Family has little influence on the country's future. (61)

43% of British women aged 15–34 would stop casual sex to reduce the risk of catching AIDS. (76)

# 44%

44% of British husbands cite their wife's adultery in their divorce proceedings. (17)

44% of British men buy their partner's underwear. (150)

44% of British females have their hair permed in any three-month period. (71)

44.2% of British high earners say that watching television is a favourite hobby. (56)

44% of British women say their men would be embarrassed if caught with their 'trousers down'. (85)

44% of British people who voted Labour in the 1987 Election were opposed to the party's non-nuclear stance. (95)

44% of British people have Sunday lunch between noon and 1.59 p.m. (111)

44% of British people say that they are eating more fish and poultry instead of red meat nowadays. (35)

44.3% of British adults who own gardens buy seeds. (154)

44% of British people feel that the Royal Family should accept valuable gifts. (161)

44% of British teenagers feel that Britain has a moral duty to offer help to the Third World. (167)

44% of British people keep letters indefinitely. (176)

44% of British men keep a wastepaper basket in their bedroom . . . 47% of women do so. (230)

44% of British men consider champagne to be the most romantic drink. (246)

44% of British divorced men believe that their own fidelity is important for a relationship to last successfully. (238)

44% of the British population have an evening meal with sausages once a week. (242)

**44% OF BRITISH PETS ARE BURIED AT THE BOTTOM OF THE GARDEN...WHEN THEY ARE DEAD. (74)**

# 45%

45% of British 15–25-year-old males feel that they might evade paying tax. (12)

45% of British 15–25-year-old males feel that they might travel on public transport without paying. (12)

45% of British housewives believe that a healthy diet should have meat at least once a day. (37)

45% of British men make their women a cup of tea in the morning. (106)

45% of British housewives are not' prepared to spend extra money on healthier food. (37)

45% of British people agree that the law should always be obeyed even if a particular law is wrong. (35)

45% of British people blame the Soviet Union for continuing the arms race. (95)

45% of British young women write cheques knowing it will put them in the red. (114)

45.5% of Britons say that if there were a General Election tomorrow, they would support the Conservative Party. (304)

45% of the British feel that large numbers of people falsely claim benefits. (35)

45% of British people feel that the most romantic gift for a woman would be a surprise weekend in Paris. (135)

45% of British fatal road accidents involving young people are linked to alcohol. (187)

45% of English blood belongs to Group O. (206)

45% of Britons have eaten their main evening meal by 6 p.m. (230)

45% of British mothers would like their sons to choose 'manual work' as a career. (255)

**Pistols are used in 45.1% of** robbery offences involving firearms in England and Wales. (265)

## OVER 45% OF HOUSEWIVES IN THE UK WHO SERVE UP AT LEAST FIVE PORTIONS OF BAKED BEANS A WEEK WATCH 'BLIND DATE'. (284)

**45%** of Britons prefer to listen to the radio during breakfast rather than talk. **(285)**

**45.8%** of Britons say they like to enjoy life and don't worry about the future. **(307)**

# 46%

46% of British women learnt the 'facts of life' from books. **(105)**

46% of British schoolgirls in England and Wales have a GCE O–level, grade A-C, in English when leaving school. **(42)**

46% of Britons want British troops to stay in Northern Ireland as long as violence continues. **(55)**

46% of British adults suffer from bruises in a 12-month period. **(175)**

46% of British people feel that, in comparison with industrial competitors, Britain is worse than most at selling goods abroad. **(35)**

46% of British people feel that farmers should produce more food and the same amount feel that the Government should withhold subsidies from farmers. **(35)**

46.6% of British children aged three or four go to school. **(17)**

When asked which they would choose first if cuts had to be made in government spending, 46% of the British population choose overseas aid. **(137)**

46% of British housewives serve frozen pizzas. **(88)**

46% of widowers remarrying in England and Wales . . . marry widows. **(202)**

46% of British men prefer their partner to be naked to make love. **(238)**

46% of British women claim that their men ask them for advice on which tie to wear on every, or almost every, occasion . . . 23% of men admit to asking their partner's opinion. **(272)**

46% of British men agree that, if a women straightens a man's tie, this is a sign that she fancies him . . . 36% of women claim that it is nothing more than wanting to be seen with a smart-looking man. **(272)**

46.8% of Britons say they love travelling abroad. **(307)**

46% of Britons agree that television programmes portray black people in inferior roles which do little to enhance their image. (295)

46% of Britons support the building of a rail tunnel link between Britain and France...41% oppose it. (327)

46% of Britons disapprove of the government's record to date. (304)

46.6% of Britons say they always buy British whenever they can. (307)

Only 46% of Britons think that BBC TV reporting is accurate. (318)

.... also, according to my new hand-held calculator, 46% of British households own a hand-held calculator,... ...and......

## 46% OF BRITISH HOUSEHOLDS OWN A HAND-HELD CALCULATOR. (154)

# 47%

47% of British marriages take place in a Registry Office. (17)

47% of second or later marriages in the United Kingdom are between couples who have both divorced. (17)

47% of British husbands claim that they frequently cook main meals whilst only *37%* of their wives claim that this is so. (144)

47% of British men always use the car for short distances. (106)

47% of British households have a table in the kitchen. (37)

47% of the total number of new residents in the UK in 1985 were British citizens. (127)

47% of British men happily eavesdrop on their partner's conversations regarding 'women's problems'. (85)

47% of British people regard Health as the highest priority for extra government spending. (35)

47% of British people say their own household's income has fallen behind prices. (35)

47% of British 40–45-year-old women wear stockings and suspenders. (172)

47% of British people would change their passport photograph if they had the chance. (145)

47% of British motorists are in favour of raising the speed limit on motorways. (208)

47% of British mothers would like to see their sons choose the armed forces as a career. (255)

47% of Britain's ethnic minority people feel that race relations in the country as a whole are worse . . . 33% of white Britons agree. (275)

# 48%

48% of British adults use a deodorant or anti-perspirant once a day. (19)

48.8% of British high earners name reading as one of the two activities to which they devote most time. (56)

48% of British pet owners visited the vet in the six months prior to interview. (74)

48% of the resident population of Great Britain are male. (156)

48% of British people think that scientists, as a breed, are... *unfashionable*. (117)

48% of the Arab population in Great Britain are aged 16–29. (127)

48% of British households have a freestanding gas cooker. (139)

48% of British people feel that women treasure diamonds above other precious stones or metals. (135)

48% of British women learnt the 'facts of life' from playground gossip. (105)

48% of British people are dissatisfied with Margaret Thatcher as Prime Minister . . . and a further 48% are satisfied. (304)

48% of British households own a hand-held hairdryer. (10)

48% of British teenagers feel that Britons have a lot to learn from Third World peoples. (167)

48% of British people watch TV on holiday and the same amount of British men watch television before dinner each evening. (162)

48% of Britons are in favour of Britain staying in the European Community. (190)

48% of Britons have difficulty finding a telephone call box that works when they wish to use one. (290)

# 49%

49% of Britons say the major topic of conversation at work is . . . work. **(285)**

49% of British couples have made love in the kitchen. **(105)**

49% of British people blame the US for continuing the arms race. **(95)**

49% of British women suffer from premenstrual tension. **(107)**

49% of British men pay the mortgage or rent for the conjugal home. **(101)**

49% of men in Great Britain work between 36 and 40 hours a week. **(17)**

49% of British brides are engaged for over one year . . . and the same number wear a long veil on their wedding day. **(211)**

49% of British employees are disturbed by 'excessive pressure in their job'. **(220)**

49% of Britain's ethnic minority people believe in tighter immigration control. **(295)**

49% of British candidates pass their driving test first time. **(8)**

49% of British 15–25-year-old males claim to eat snacks rather than main meals. **(12)**

49% of British people feel that food that is healthy is usually more expensive. **(35)**

49% of British households own a pet. **(18)**

49% of British men say that a friendly smile attracts them physically to their partner. **(246)**

49% of British men consider strawberries to be the most romantic food. **(246)**

49% of British men agree that women are better at choosing ties than men. **(272)**

# 50%

## 50% OF BRITISH OVER-65-YEAR-OLDS CONSIDER LOVEMAKING A SOLUTION TO THE COLD OF WINTER. (204)

**50%** of British teenagers eat chips up to five times a week. (2)

**50%** of British women aged 15–34 years say they would buy condoms for their boyfriend. (76)

**50%** of British women have tried making love in front of a mirror. (105)

**50%** of British people believe the arms race will continue unabated. (95)

**50%** of British women over 35 years feel that a man expects them to 'repay' him for the first date by leaping into bed. (112)

**50%** of British people feel that a happy sexual relationship is very important to a successful marriage. (35)

50% of British people think that scientists as a breed are in touch with everyday life. (117)

50% of British men choose black when buying sexy lingerie for their partners. (150)

Over 50% of Pakistani or Bangladeshi households in Great Britain contain five or more people. (127)

50% of British people feel that the design and colour of frames is important when buying new spectacles. (134)

50% of Britain's unemployed smoke. (297)

50% of Britons agree that, except to preserve a mother's life, abortion, is morally wrong and any limits on it are a good thing. (311)

50% of British women borrow their partner's razors to shave their legs. (1)

50% of British teenagers say they feel miserable or depressed most or all of the time. (2)

50% of British people feel that Prince Harry and Prince William should stay in private education. (161)

50% of British drivers fail the driving test first time. (170)

Over 50% of Britons have not heard of the CEGB. (193)

50% of Britons tune in to Her Majesty the Queen's Christmas Broadcast. (202)

Under 50% of British 8–14-year-olds know what happened in 1066. (228)

50% of British households have the facility of a shower. (240)

50% of British men would like to spend Valentine's Day with Samantha Fox. (246)

50% of British women believe in astrology. (225)

50% of Britain's ethnic minorities are Christian. (275)

50% of British men say they make the bed in the morning. (285)

**51% OF BRITISH WOMEN WISH THEIR MEN WERE MORE PASSIONATE. (82)**

# 51%

51% of British 15–25-year-old males believe that in times of high unemployment women should lose their job first. **(12)**

51.8% of British women use nail varnish. **(88)**

51% of British adults do not consider making changes to the lighting when redecorating. **(28)**

51.3% of babies born in England and Wales in 1986 were male. **(38)**

51% of British men like to spend their leisure hours with their women. **(106)**

51% of British households have made no conscious decision to revise their diet as a result of publicity on healthy eating. **(40)**

51% of the West Indian population in Britain were born in the UK. **(51)**

51% of British women expect their male partner to be able to make love to them more than once in the same evening. **(105)**

51% of British men decide when love-making is over for the night. **(105)**

51% of homicide cases in England and Wales occur as a result of quarrel, revenge or loss of temper. **(265)**

51% of British women claim that they do not bitch about their men to friends when the relationship is going through a bad patch. **(84)**

51% of British couples pool all their money and each takes out what he/she needs. **(35)**

51% of British women under 20 years learnt the 'facts of life' from their mother. **(105)**

51% of British single men believe that their girlfriends usually reach orgasm through intercourse ... whereas only 24% of single girls say this is true. **(238)**

51% of British mothers would like their sons to choose the police force as a career. **(255)**

# 52%

52% of the British population are women. (78)

52% of British people feel that, in comparison with industrial competitors, Britain is better than most at inventing new products. (35)

52% of British deaths by fire are linked to alcohol. (187)

52% of British men prefer to shop with a wife or girlfriend in tow. (97)

52% of Britons think that telephone charges are unreasonable. (290)

52% of British households hung wallpaper in their last home decorating task. (113)

52% of British people do not think that the NHS offers value for money to the taxpayer. (132)

52% of British people dislike Mrs Thatcher. (137)

52% of British men claim to know their partner's correct waist and bust sizes. (150)

52% of British weddings in England and Wales involve a religious ceremony. (202)

52% of British car purchasers bought imported cars in 1987. (223)

52% of Britons think that judges should be able to give the death sentence in the case of major drug dealers. (231)

52% of British men say they have wondered about going to a prostitute. (238)

52% of British men consider a four poster to be the most romantic honeymoon bed. (246)

52% of British housewives, if given the choice between an extra hour's work a day from their man, or a new domestic machine, would choose a machine. (273)

52% of British housewives are heavy users of toilet paper. (88)

52% of British people do not go to the dentist. (57)

# 53%

53% of British couples argue over money. (101)

53% of Scottish men prefer to spend their leisure hours in front of the television. (106)

53% of British top earners (£25,000+ annual household income) say that tax motivates them to earn more. (56)

53% of British company executives receive subsidized lunches. (185)

53% of British women say they would never practise *postillionage* with their men. (105)

53.7% of British adults suffered from sore throats in the last 12 months. (88)

53% of Britons think that Neil Kinnock is not proving a good leader of the Labour Party. (304)

53% of British motorists are in favour of liberalizing pub hours. (208)

53% of British weddings are recorded on video. (211)

53% of British adults say they would obey the law without exception. (227)

53% of all children killed or injured on British roads are pedestrians. (232)

53% of British children say that their fathers shout at other drivers. (305)

53% of Britain's ethnic minority people consider their housing to be worse than that for white people ... 4% consider it better. (275)

# 54%

54% of British households own a bicycle. (22)

54% of British 15–25-year-old females have a bank account. (12)

54% of British men make their own dental, hairdressing or doctor's appointments. (106)

54% of British 15–25-year-old males feel it is wrong to get divorced. (12)

54% of British adults regard Ronald Reagan unfavourably. (103)

54% of British men do not bother to iron their own shirt if they get up first in the morning and find it creased. (106)

54% of British spectacle wearers own only one pair. (110)

54.7% of British women use knitting yarn and wool. (88)

54% of British men prefer women to wear briefs ... as opposed to other styles of underwear. (150)

54% of British wives claim that their husbands never do the main food shopping while *only 48%* of their husbands claim that this is so. (144)

54% of Britons are in favour of the names of those convicted of drink-driving being broadcast on television. (210)

54% of British men agree that when a man goes to a mirror and straightens his tie he's using his tie as an excuse to have a quick look at himself. (272)

54% of British men are partially clothed when they shave in the morning. (285)

54% of Britons under 24 think that they and their partner will stay together for ever. (287)

54.3% of Britons agree that they are perfectly happy with their standard of living. (307)

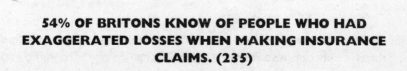

So let's get this right.
The thieves took one Rembrandt,
one diamond tiara, a set of
wedgwood, a.......

INSURANCE
CLAIMS

**54% OF BRITONS KNOW OF PEOPLE WHO HAD
EXAGGERATED LOSSES WHEN MAKING INSURANCE
CLAIMS. (235)**

# 55%

## 55% OF BRITISH MEN SLEEP IN THE NUDE. (90)

**55%** of British men under 24 say they think more highly of virgins. **(287)**

**55.8%** of Britons agree that it is important to be attractive to the opposite sex whatever your age. **(307)**

**55%** of British mothers would like their sons to enter the fire brigade as a career. **(255)**

**55%** of the British white population agree that it is more difficult for ethnic-minority people to get jobs than it is for whites. **(275)**

**55%** of British people say that fear of burglary/mugging is the most worrying aspect of their daily life. (113)

**55%** of British households own an electric toaster. (37)

**55%** of British boys under 15 years help their mothers in the kitchen. (40)

**55%** of British customers feel that a false smile is better than no smile at all. (7)

**55%** of British pet owners think that pets are better company than humans. (74)

**55%** of British men leave their dirty clothes on the floor. (106)

**55%** of British women think that men are far more interested in sexual conquest than establishing an emotional relationship. (112)

**55%** of Britons feel that living apart from in-laws is very important to a successful marriage. (35)

**55%** of victims of fatal accidents occurring in British homes are over 75 years. (136)

**55%** of British adults have at least one credit commitment. (138)

**55%** of British women say they would never try making love in front of a video camera. (105)

**55%** of British women prefer their men to shave before coming to bed. (1)

**55%** of British people wear spectacles. (110)

**55%** of British people use hairspray. (71)

# 56%

56% of British married men say they always or usually make the first move sexually . . . only 4% of wives usually make the first move. (238)

56% of British fathers believe that having children has had a good effect on their marriage in general. (238)

56% of Britons think that the present limit on legal abortion should be reduced from 28 weeks. (247)

56% of British women aged 75 and over live alone. (263)

56% of British couples like saying 'naughty' things to each other in bed. (105)

56.5% of British adults suffered from coughs in the last 12 months. (88)

56% of British women think hairy faces make men look older. (1)

56% of British men get angry when their partners borrow their razors to shave their legs. (1)

56% of Britons agree that trade unions are out of touch with the workers they represent. (67)

56% of London tube drivers find their work pleasant. (171)

56% of the British population were regular book readers in 1987. (233)

56% of British 15–25-year-old females feel it is wrong to get divorced. (12)

56% of British women say that they have regular dental check-ups. (42)

56.5% of British women say they enjoy entertaining at home. (307)

56.5% of British women say their men leave the bathroom door open . . . when they are in the bathroom. (85)

56% of British people wash their hair while in the bath. (230)

56% of British women leave the signing of legal documentation to their men. (100)

**56%** of British women say their husbands do DIY jobs at least once a week. (230)

**56%** of British people say that scientists, as a breed, are too secretive. (117)

**56%** of British high earners (£25,000+ annual household income) own a top label garment. (56)

**56.2%** of British adults buy petrol. (88)

**56%** of Britons say they are unlikely to inform police if they are offered stolen goods. (325)

**56%** of the British clergy are in favour of women priests. (168)

**56%** of British women feel that their man helps more around the house than their father did. (96)

**56%** of British 15–25-year-old males rate good health first as a constituent of happiness. (12)

**56%** of British people say that, compared to two or three years ago, they are eating more grilled food instead of fried food. (35)

# 57%

57% of British people do not agree that the poll tax should be paid by every adult in the house. **(9)**

57% of British 20–25-year-olds strongly agree that immigration should be more restricted. **(12)**

57% of British women describe their GPs as 'sympathetic and reassuring'. **(115)**

57% of British people feel that modern farming damages the countryside. **(35)**

57.5% of British women say they sometimes treat themselves to something they don't need. **(307)**

57% of British men sulk. **(102)**

57% of British young women describe their bank managers as *helpful.* **(114)**

57% of British men say they go to bed at the same time as their wife . . . whereas 51% of British women say they go to bed at the same time as their husband. **(230)**

57% of British husbands spend £75 or more on their wives at Christmas. **(135)**

57% of British adults suffer from tiredness in a 12-month period. **(175)**

57% of British dogs have a pedigree. **(188)**

57% of British dogs are owned by women. **(188)**

57% of British women say that their chief cause of stress is money. **(254)**

57% of British mothers would like their sons and daughters to choose journalism as a career. **(255)**

57% of British men are only concerned about whether clothes *fit* when they are buying them. **(97)**

57% of men released from prison in England and Wales are reconvicted within two years. **(282)**

**Only** 57% of the British public find royal news very, or fairly, interesting. **(277)**

# 58%

58% of British 15–25-year-old males have a bank account. (12)

58% of British households do not watch breakfast television while having breakfast. (40)

58% of British children say that their fathers, while driving, vent their frustrations on their horn. (305)

58.8% of British men suffered headaches in the last 12 months. (88)

**58% OF BRITONS SAY THEY WOULD CHALLENGE SOMEONE WHO TRIED TO JUMP A QUEUE. (259)**

**58%** of British men clip their toenails regularly. **(106)**

**58.9%** of British men use talcum powder. **(88)**

**58%** of home accident victims in England and Wales are male. **(232)**

**58%** of all Britons say they would find it acceptable if a member of their family married someone from a different racial background. **(300)**

**58%** of British women think that Princess Diana is the best-dressed of all female royal personalities. **(245)**

**58%** of British 15–25-year-old females rate health first as a constituent of happiness. **(12)**

**58%** of Britons think that Channel 4 contains 'a lot of sex'. **(326)**

**58%** of British people think that the job of a traffic warden is one of the worst. **(7)**

**58%** of British women think their men are prone to the odd lie. **(87)**

**58%** of Welshmen never clean the lavatory. **(96)**

**58%** of British men buy the right size underwear for their partners. **(150)**

**58%** of British wine drinkers buy wine from a supermarket. **(41)**

**58%** of British teenage boys have a television set in their own bedroom...50% of girls have one too. **(317)**

# 59%

59% of British people feel that a major accident at a British nuclear power station within the next ten years is likely. (35)

59% of British householders do not intend to fit any security devices in their homes in the next year. (113)

59% of British Conservatives feel that there is very little real poverty in Britain. (35)

59% of British people feel that consistent over-drinking is sufficient reason for divorce. (35)

59% of British people feel that the Royal Family should be free to say whatever they like to the Press. (163)

59% of British single clergy say they are against the ordination of women. (168)

59% of British women think their men have actually grown more affectionate as the years have gone by. (276)

59% of Britons believe that more MPs from ethnic minorities would help to ease racial tensions. (300)

59% of British 15–25-year-old females feel that divorce may happen to them. (12)

59% of unmarried Britons feel that society ought to do more to safeguard marriage. (35)

59% of British women describe their man as 'unbeatable' or 'wonderful' between the sheets. (319)

59% of British men experience diminished libido after an argument with their partner. (112)

59% of British customers do not always complain when they get bad service. (7)

59% of British couples make love once or twice a week. (82)

59% of British households have an electric drill. (139)

# 60%

60.1% of British people drink 1.71 cups of coffee a day. (109)

60% of British men are trying to open up emotionally. (112)

60.8% of Britons agree that they like spending most of their time at home with the family. (307)

60% of women in Great Britain work between 36 and 40 hours a week. (17)

60% of British people shut their eyes when kissing in a romantic clinch. (89)

60% of British nurses work unpaid overtime. (133)

60% of fatal accidents occurring in British homes are due to falls. (136)

60% of British women say they bath or shower every day...and 60% of women share a bath with their man. (286)

60% of British people are dressed when they eat breakfast. (160)

60% of the British white population is over 29 years of age. (33)

60% of the British Asian population is under 29 years of age. (33)

60% of British businesswomen travelling alone report some form of unpleasant experience. (32)

60% of Britons agree that TV violence gives children the impression that murder occurs daily. (328)

60% of British women say they are starved of romance. (337)

60% of British housewives do not have the use of a car during the week. (65)

60% of British women say they would never make love with more than one man during the course of an evening. (105)

60% of British people think that Prince Edward's decision to quit the Marines and pursue another career was the right one. (161)

## 60% OF BRITISH PEOPLE OVER 65 YEARS WOULD PREFER TO TAKE HOT BUBBLE BATHS ALONE. (204)

**60%** of Britain's 'eligible' older men see their ideal woman driving a reliable, practical car. **(342)**

**60%** of British single men say that 'a sense of humour' is an important characteristic for them to feel attracted to a possible partner. **(238)**

**60%** of British men in steady relationships (including marriage) want to make love more often. **(238)**

**60%** of British couples occasionally look at erotic material. **(238)**

**60%** of British women say that they can reach multiple orgasms. **(105)**

**60%** of British women say they see no wrong in having children out of wedlock. **(255)**

# 61%

61% of British women in Northern Ireland are happy with their men's bottoms. (83)

61% of British women think their men are generous. (86)

61% of the adult population in England and Wales have married. (127)

61% of British people dislike their passport photograph. (145)

61% of British clergy say that practising homosexual clergy should be warned to refrain from such acts. (168)

61% of London's tube drivers find their work interesting. (171)

61% of British adults eat foods that are high in fibre. (175)

61% of British men keep a radio in the bedroom. (230)

61% of British people agree that their bathroom accessories must match the colour of their bathroom suite. (240)

61% of British television viewers are against programmes for, about or by homosexuals. (244)

61% of white Britons agree that in times of high unemployment it is ethnic minority people who are most likely to be unable to get jobs. (275)

61% of Britons, as a crime prevention measure, do not carry large amounts of cash. (4)

61% of British households watch television during the evening meal. (40)

# 62%

**62%** of British men would be pleased and gratified if their partner had a better-paid or more prestigious job than them. **(112)**

**62%** of British people would rather don an extra sweater than hop into bed with someone special or have a double brandy. **(47)**

**61% OF BRITISH PEOPLE BELIEVE THAT EVEN IF A NUCLEAR WAR IS NOT DELIBERATELY STARTED, AN ACCIDENT WILL HAPPEN. (95)**

62% of Britons would like to know more about the European Parliament. (190)

62% of British husbands say they *never* have any difficulty becoming sexually aroused. (238)

62% of British adults suffered from severe headaches in the last 12 months. (88)

62% of British housewives use window cleaners. (88)

62% of Britain's ethnic minority people feel that they have worse relations with the police than white people. (275)

62% of Britons say they are far less likely to have a one night stand now than before the AIDS crisis. (288)

62% of Britons judge the police to be honest. (312)

62% of British women reckon that men look sexy in underwear. (150)

62% of British 15–25-year-old females believe that women should fight for total equality. (12)

62% of British households have a car. (51)

62% of British men would not kill a spider in the bath – they'd scoop it up and put it outside. (99)

62% of serious head injuries to British males are linked to alcohol. (187)

**62% OF BRITONS ARE AGAINST THE INTRODUCTION OF CONDOM MACHINES IN SCHOOLS. (182)**

# 63%

63% of British women wish their men would improve their seduction routines. (82)

63% of the thriftiest men in Britain are from . . . Scotland. (86)

63% of British women enjoy their work. (107)

63% of British men expect their women to 'go Dutch' after their first date. (112)

63% of British female patients who are registered with a male GP say they would rather see a woman doctor. (115)

63% of British housewives claim that their husbands help with the washing-up on most days . . . while 73% of their husbands claim that this is so. (144)

63% of Britons believe that crime is understandable if people are in difficult circumstances such as unemployment. (325)

63% of British marriages in England and Wales are between bachelors and spinsters. (202)

63% of British women say they are contented with their own sexual attractiveness. (254)

63% of British mothers would like their daughters to choose nursing as a career. (255)

63.5% of Britons say they can't bear untidiness in the house. (307)

63% of Britons agree that abortion is used too often as a means of birth control. (311)

63% of British people aged over 50 say they do not drink. (116)

63% of British women prefer to buy their own underwear. (150)

# 64%

**64%** of British men who buy their partner's underwear choose 'sexy' outfits. **(150)**

**64%** of British motorists are in favour of unrestricted power of the police to stop and breathalyse anyone in charge of a vehicle. **(208)**

**64%** of British married men having affairs say they do so simply because the opportunity presents itself. **(238)**

**64%** of Scottish men take turns in changing the sheets. **(90)**

**64%** of British women take the Pill. **(107)**

**64%** of British men snore. **(90)**

**64%** of British men *never* have a cup of tea or coffee when they wake in the morning . . . nor do 59% of women. **(285)**

*Oh No! Not the bloody time of the month again!*

## 65% OF BRITISH WOMEN SUFFERING PRE-MENSTRUAL SYNDROME SAY THEY GET VERY DEPRESSED AT THIS TIME OF THE MONTH. (149)

# 65%

65% of British teetotallers are women. (116)

65% of British women say they have good skin. (107)

65% of British people do not agree with privatization of the electricity and water industries. (9)

65% of British 15–25-year-old males agree that everybody should be tested for the AIDS virus. (12)

65% of British girls under 15 years help their mothers in the kitchen. (40)

65% of British men sweeten their beverages. (109)

65% of British people expect unemployment to have risen in a year from now (1986). (35)

65% of British teenagers believe that developing countries should not imitate Britain but go their own way. (167)

65% of British people who drink and drive say they could drive as safely or more safely after drinking as they could before. (208)

65.4% of British adults have a current driving licence. (88)

65% of British employees say that work flows smoothly in their department. (220)

Only 65% of Britons eligible in 1984 for family income supplement took it up. (263)

65% of deaths of British 15–19 year-olds are caused by accidents and violence. (232)

65% of British men say that the first thing they do in the morning is ... wash ... 79% of women do this. (285)

# 66%

66% of British 15–25-year-old females agree that everybody should be tested for the AIDS virus. (12)

66% of British housewives say that breakfast is the most important meal of the day. (37)

66% of British women suffered headaches over the last 12 months. (88)

66% of British women say their men are less narrow-minded now than they were when they first met. (85)

66% of British women are over 5ft 4ins. (107)

66% of British people feel that political parties are interested only in people's votes, not in their opinions. (35)

66% of British women keep secrets from their men. (87)

66.2% of British adults suffered colds in the last 12 months. (88)

66% of British men remember their women's birthdays. (106)

66% of British couples put their possessions in their joint names. (112)

66% of British people agree that censorship of films and magazines is necessary to uphold moral standards. (35)

66% of British women given sexy lingerie will wear it when their partner will see it. (150)

66% of British employees think their company is 'well managed'. (220)

66% of Alliance voters regularly read books in 1987, as opposed to 55% of Tories and 51% of Labour voters. (233)

66% of British television viewers think that the National Front should not be allowed to make a programme arguing for compulsory repatriation of blacks. (244)

66% of British voters are in favour of retaining a mix of state and private health provision. (249)

**66%** of British 15–25-year-old males feel that divorce may happen to them. **(12)**

**66%** of British women want the right to end their own lives if fatally ill. **(255)**

**66%** of British babies were vaccinated against whooping cough in 1986. **(263)**

**66%** of Britons claim they are never late for work. **(285)**

**66%** of Britons believe showering is more hygienic than bathing . . . 10% insist that bathing is cleaner. **(286)**

**66%** of Britons under 24 think that the current trend is towards fewer sexual relationships with very special sexual partners . . . only 24% consider more relationships to be the trend. **(287)**

**66.3%** of Britons agree that their family is more important to them than their career. **(307)**

**66%** of British teenagers drink alcohol during the week to overcome nervousness and shyness. **(2)**

**66%** of Britons agree that young people today don't have enough respect for traditional British values. **(35)**

**66%** of British parents let their child have a say in decision-making. **(35)**

# 67%

67% of British adults think that the BBC is well run. (227)

67% of British women say that the size of their partner's sex organ is not important. (105)

67% of British men usually send romantic Valentine's cards. (246)

67% of white Britons say they have never minded ethnic minorities being in Britain . . . 8% say that they have always minded. (275)

67% of British men say they do not take into account what the weather forecasts have said when they get dressed in the morning . . . nor do 57% of women. (285)

67% of British adults buy extra strong mints . . . 43% of them do it every week. (298)

67% of British men say they never discuss their sex life outside the home. (301)

67% of Britons think that people are less polite than they were at the beginning of the 1980s. (304)

67% of Britons think that over the last eight years or so our towns and cities have become less tidy and dirtier than they were. (304)

67% of Britons feel that parents should try to teach children respect for other people. (35)

67% of Britons believe that battery cage production of chickens should be banned. (178)

67% of British brides think that children are an essential part of marriage. (211)

67% of British bridegrooms asked their fiancée's father's permission to marry. (211)

67% of British men will stand up for a lady's honour if a stranger becomes abusive. (48)

**67%** of Scots wear spectacles. **(110)**

**67%** of British young women aged 15–35 say doctors should issue free condoms. **(76)**

**67%** of British women say they have fantasized about other men while making love. **(105)**

**67%** of British women would *never* encourage their man to fantasize about other women while making love. **(105)**

I sold his body to medicine but decided to keep his mind.

**67% OF BRITISH WOMEN SAY THEY ARE MORE IN LOVE WITH THEIR MAN'S MIND THAN HIS BODY. (83)**

# 68%

68% of British women describe their men's fingernails as always well manicured. (90)

68% of British adults regard Mr Gorbachov favourably. (103)

68% of British people taking domestic self-catering holidays, go to bed earlier, sleep better and get up later. (162)

68% of British people have holidayed abroad. (162)

68% of the British clergy feel that clergymen should not be Freemasons. (168)

68% of British married men wish their partner made the first move sexually more often. (238)

68% of Britons believe homosexuals should not be allowed to demonstrate affection in public. (315)

68% of Britons disagree that the National Health Service is safe in the hands of the Conservatives. (321)

68% of British men gossip. (84)

68% of British women are happy with their male partner's attitude to love-making. (105)

68% of Britons think that punctuality is important. (259)

68% of Britons drink tea at breakfast. (285)

68% of British women say their men hold the door open for them. (319)

**68% OF BRITISH MEN DISAPPROVE OF THEIR WOMEN SWEARING. (85)**

# 69%

**69%** of British car owners claim to hand-wash their cars at weekends. **(338)**

**69%** of British women use some form of contraception. **(107)**

**69%** of British women aged 15–34 years believe there should be compulsory AIDS screening. **(75)**

**69%** of British teenagers have seen a 'video nasty' or pornographic video. **(2)**

**69%** of British people feel that Britain should keep its nuclear weapons until it has persuaded others to reduce theirs. **(35)**

**69%** of British people feel that understanding and tolerance are very important to a successful marriage. **(35)**

**69%** of British households have central heating. **(51)**

**69%** of British women say they would never make love with another woman. **(105)**

**69%** of British people think the Conservatives will win the next General Election. **(137)**

**69%** of couples in England and Wales marrying for the first time prefer to walk down the aisle. **(202)**

**69%** of British men do not know how to tie a 'dickie bow'. **(272)**

**69%** of British men say they take under 30 minutes for lunch on weekdays. **(285)**

**69%** of Britons say that the AIDS crisis is responsible for the trend towards fewer sexual relationships. **(288)**

# 70%

70% of British consumers say that if a service is particularly good, they wouldn't mind too much if the goods were a little more expensive. (7)

70% of British women say they would not believe a man who said he was taking the Pill. (215)

70% of British women believe that there is life after death. (255)

70% of British people always wash their hands after using the lavatory. (46)

70% of British men over 65 years are forced to get up one or more times a night to empty their bladders. (152)

70% of British smokers want to give up. (92)

70% of British nurses who have second jobs say they are forced to seek extra work for money reasons. (133)

70% of British dog owners believe their pet knows it's Christmas. (50)

70% of British people feel that, generally speaking, those they elect as MPs lose touch with people pretty quickly. (35)

70% of UK brides acquire a new diamond engagement ring. (165)

Almost 70% of British 17-year-olds say they should get their sex education from their parents rather than teachers. (2)

70% of Britons say they have not heard of Britoil. (193)

70% of British motorists agree that manufacturers of alcoholic drinks should put a government 'Don't Drink and Drive' warning on their products. (208)

70% of British motorists do not trust garages in general. (217)

70% of British consumers have not made a complaint for five years . . . 62% wish they had. (299)

70% of Britons clean their teeth before going to bed. (230)

**70%** of Britons agree that it would be wrong to change the abortion law so that women were forced to give birth to handicapped babies. **(311)**

**70%** of British women say they think of their husband as their best friend. **(250)**

**70%** of British women admit to petty theft at work. **(253)**

**Over 70%** of British people prefer the word 'knickers' to 'pants' . . . when referring to underwear. **(150)**

**70%** of British women say that they prefer clean-shaven men. **(1)**

**70%** of British housewives claim their husbands know where everything in the kitchen is kept. **(37)**

Hi, sex kitten! Was I good last night or was I good? . . . Oh, sorry, Mrs Finch, is your Mandy there?

**70% OF BRITISH MEN TELEPHONE THEIR WOMEN SOON AFTER THEY HAVE SLEPT TOGETHER FOR THE FIRST TIME. (112)**

# 71%

71% of the British clergy agree that the Church can never approve of homosexual acts. (168)

71% of British motorists believe that a driver who fails a breath test should be immediately disqualified from driving. (208)

71% of British men have a bedside lamp in their bedroom. (230)

71% of British men who have partners say they masturbate at least occasionally. (238)

71% of British housewives use butter. (88)

71% of British women rate their love lives as good, very good or excellent. (105)

71% of British people agree with the statement 'you never know what's in a sausage.' (242)

71% of British women say that poor personal grooming and hygiene turn them off most about the male sex. (245)

71% of British people think that the average MP has little influence on the country's future. (61)

71% of the British population regard trade unions as a good thing. (67)

71% of British men use razor blades. (88)

71% of British women are in favour of contraceptive advertising on TV and radio. (146)

71.9% of British adults grow flowers. (154)

71% of British people believe that the advantages of the Royal Family outweigh the cost. (163)

71% of British working mothers say that they feel guilty about not being a full-time mother. (254)

71% of white Britons believe in tighter immigration control. (295)

71% of Britons approve of an abortion being carried out when a woman has been raped. (280)

# 72%

72% of British people feel that it is the government's responsibility to reduce income differences between rich and poor. (35)

72% of British people feel that parents should try to teach children good manners. (35)

72% of British males read a daily newspaper. (125)

72% of the British population aged 25–29 years hold an educational qualification. (126)

72% of British men are in favour of contraceptive advertising on TV and radio. (146)

72% of British companies do not give their employees any free holidays at Christmas. (151)

72% of Britons take their home holidays by the sea. (162)

72% of Britons taking villa holidays in Spain bring their own tea from home. (322)

72% of British adults think that the police force is well run. (227)

72% of British people spend no more than £4 on a pair of knickers. (150)

72% of British people agree that those who break the law should be given stiffer sentences. (35)

72% of British women say that they have 'gone in for love bites'. (105)

72% of British men use aftershave lotion. (88)

72% of British men always reach a climax when they make love. (238)

72% of British men have a driving licence. (263)

72% of British women who have a bank overdraft say that it was pre-arranged. (114)

# 73%

73% of British households have loft insulation. **(139)**

73% of British people think capital punishment should be reintroduced. **(231)**

73% of British people feel that experts contradict each other over what makes a healthy diet. **(35)**

73% of British housewives use plain flour. **(131)**

73% of British women read a Sunday newspaper. **(125)**

73% of British women under 20 expect a man to be able to have intercourse more than once in the same evening. **(105)**

73% of British women say they don't mind either *giving* or *receiving* a kiss. **(89)**

**73% OF BRITISH WOMEN SAY THEY ARE PERFECTLY HAPPY WITH THEIR MEN'S HEIGHT. (83)**

73% of British people think junior members of the Royal Family should pursue careers. **(161)**

73% of British clergy believe that Christ was born of a Virgin. **(168)**

73% of British adults rate their health as 'above average'. **(175)**

73% of British people took at least two holidays away from home in the last five years. **(162)**

73% of British non-manual workers mix socially with their colleagues. **(285)**

# 74%

74% of British couples have tried saying 'naughty' things to each other in bed. (105)

74% of British women say they always know where their men are...and with whom. (87)

74% of Britons vote the British cup of tea the best in the world. (109)

74% of British couples have tried making love in the bath. (105)

74% of British people think that scientists as a breed are responsible. (117)

74% of British couples describe their weekends as enjoyable. (60)

74% of British teenagers feel that Britain should help the poorest countries. (167)

74% of Britons think that Britain's road network needs improving. (210)

74% of British men who make love every day say they are happy with their sex lives. (238)

74% of Britons who have had private medical treatment say it was better than the NHS. (260)

# 75%

75% of British men say they like to have DIY equipment for Christmas. (50)

75% of British people say they would never dream of going out without underwear. (150)

75% of British people believe that a mother with a child under five years should not work at all outside the home. (66)

75% of British women aged between 15 and 34 say they would stick to one partner because of AIDS. (76)

75% of British people feel that Britain should remain a member of NATO. (35)

75% of British householders used gloss paint in their last DIY decorating task. (113)

75% of British viewers say they would not pay for cable TV. (119)

75% of British people feel that the highest government priority should be given to keeping down unemployment. (35)

75% of Britons think that the current driving test should include some instruction on motorway driving. (210)

75% of Britons finish their evening meal in less than 30 minutes and sit at the same place at the table. (230)

75% of British accidental deaths occur on the roads or in the home. (232)

75% of British women who have used a vibrator say they liked the experience. (105)

75% of British voters feel that private medicine should not be abolished. (249)

75% of British women do not think of themselves as feminists, although nearly all believe in equal rights. (250)

75% of British tie-wearing men say that straightening an already perfect tie is a sure sign of nervousness. (272)

**75%** of British children say that their fathers get cross with other drivers. **(305)**

**75%** of British people feel that ceasing to love the other is sufficient reason for divorce. **(35)**

**75%** of the British population are Protestant. **(157)**

**75%** of British MPs say that they receive letters which influence their own views...yet 75% of British MPs find up to 20% of the letters they receive difficult to understand. **(177)**

**75%** of British 17-year-olds favour capital punishment for serious crimes...and flogging for football hooligans. **(2)**

**75%** of Britons think that judges should be able to give the death sentence in the case of murders of policemen. **(231)**

**75% OF BRITISH MEN WOULD RATHER KEEP THEIR TREASURED CHILDHOOD MEMORIES – CRICKET BATS AND TEDDY BEARS – THAN HAVE THEM THROWN AWAY. (99)**

# 76%

76% of men in the South-West and Midlands say they haven't a clue what to do with an iron. (96)

76% of British men remember special occasions and mark them with a gift or romantic gesture. (112)

76% of British men buy jewellery for their women to say 'I love you.' (135)

76% of British women say they enjoy fellatio. (105)

76% of British MPs count Sunday Trading as one of the topical issues people write to them about most frequently. (177)

76% of British company executives receive free medical insurance. (185)

76% of British brides use, or plan to use the Pill. (211)

76% of Britons watch television once the evening meal is over. (230)

76% of Britons do not think that men are less well mannered than women. (259)

It's such a lovely day I thought I'd come and have my ears syringed

SURGERY

**76% OF BRITISH WOMEN CONSULT A GP AT LEAST ONCE DURING A 12-MONTH PERIOD. (38)**

# 77%

77% of British people feel that those with higher incomes should pay a much larger proportion in taxes compared with those with lower incomes. **(35)**

77% of British people feel that farmers look after the countryside well. **(35)**

77.6% of British housewives serve corned beef. **(88)**

77% of British cat owners use cat litter at some stage. **(283)**

77% of British adults claim that they eat a diet that is well balanced. **(175)**

77% of British people feel that Britain would be worse off without the Royals. **(161)**

77% of British telephone owners write personal letters...whilst only 66% of those without a telephone do so. **(176)**

77% of British men rate their partners as a good or excellent lover...4% of married men say she's downright poor. **(238)**

77% of British married men had sex with their wives before marriage. **(238)**

77% of consumer durables in Britain are bought with credit cards. **(278)**

77% of Britons feel that racial tensions would be eased by recruiting more ethnic policemen. **(300)**

# 78%

**78%** of British 15–25-year-old females feel they might have sex outside marriage. **(12)**

**78%** of British women admit to spending self-indulgently. **(101)**

**78%** of British top earners (£25,000+ annual household income) have two cars. **(56)**

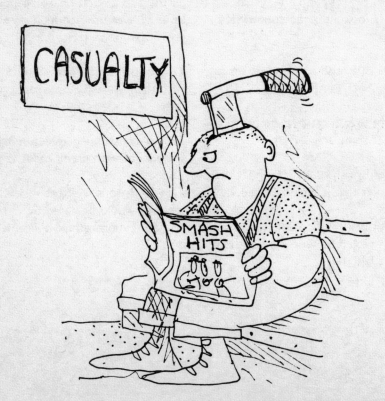

**78.7% OF BRITISH READERS OF *SMASH HITS* SUFFERED HEADACHES IN THE LAST 12 MONTHS. (88)**

78% of British couples talk during love play. (105)

78% of British men read a Sunday newspaper. (125)

78% of British employees are in employment. (155)

78% of the Church of England clergy are satisfied with the Archbishop of Canterbury's leadership of the Church. (168)

78% of British housewives use air fresheners. (88)

78% of British company executives receive five weeks' annual holiday. (185)

78% of British 'captains of industry' regularly read the *Sunday Times*. (234)

78% of British single men say that it is men who are still usually expected to make the first move to start a relationship. (238)

78% of British women say they can talk openly and honestly with their men about their sexual desires. (82)

**78.9% OF BRITISH HOUSEWIVES SERVE FROZEN PEAS. (88)**

# 79%

79% of British women would like to make love to their partner more often. **(82)**

79% of Britons say they are very happy with their spouse. **(230)**

79% of British people, in the weeks following the Chernobyl accident, felt that nuclear power stations create serious risk for the future. **(35)**

79% of British 17–24-year-olds vote the traditional pub as their favourite place. **(94)**

79% of British workers identify strongly with their employers. **(189)**

79% of Britons who have a take-away meal while watching videos choose a Chinese meal. **(205)**

79% of Britons aged 25–34 say that it could be the woman who makes the first move to go out with a partner...19% think it should be the man. **(288)**

79% of Britons agree that those making the decision to have an abortion – men as well as women – may suffer severely from guilt afterwards, especially if the abortion is carried out late in the pregnancy after the baby has been felt moving. **(311)**

# 80%

80% of British households own a washing machine. (24)

80% of British people over 90 are women. (38)

80% of British women say they prefer jewellery to lingerie as Christmas presents. (50)

80% of British people look forward to Christmas. (50)

80% of British men say they love to receive jewellery as presents. (50)

80% of British women read horoscopes. (255)

80% of British men agree that wearing spectacles makes no difference at all to a woman's attractiveness. (110)

80% of Britons think that judges should be able to give the death sentence in the case of murders committed by terrorists. (231)

80% of British women say that they knew how much was in their bank account at the time of survey. (114)

80% of British people agree that workers should be given more say in running the places where they work. (35)

80% of the British working population pass a bakery outlet on their way to work. (131)

80% of British women claim they are faithful to their partners. (332)

80% of Britons have never been inside an aeroplane. (340)

80% of British teachers say that they have been subjected to offensive verbal abuse. (169)

80% of British 40–45-year-old women wear jeans. (172)

80% of Britons donate to charity. (195)

80% of British pub customers demand an extension on closing time each night from 11p.m. to midnight. (309)

# 81%

81% of Britons approve of GPs retiring at 70. **(137)**

81% of British households have not considered buying their 'council house'. **(51)**

81% of British men in Wales gossip. **(84)**

81% of British men say that they did not receive enough sexual education at school. **(238)**

81.7% of British women use lipstick. **(88)**

81% of Britons agree that the government should give a much higher priority to protecting the environment. **(191)**

81% of British brides are married in white. **(211)**

81.5% of British housewives use scouring pads. **(88)**

**81% OF BRITISH PET OWNERS BELIEVE THAT BY STROKING A PET THEY CAN REDUCE STRESS AND TENSION THEY MAY BE FEELING. (74)**

# 82%

82% of British people buy three pairs of knickers at a time. (150)

82% of British women do not tell their partners they have been using their razors to shave their legs. (1)

82% of British women consider men wimpish when it comes to emotions. (48)

82% of British people drink 3.73 cups of tea a day. (109)

82% of British women report that their men are sometimes gallant. (112)

82% of British people say their partners would never go out without underwear. (150)

82% of British people feel that Prince Charles should speak out on controversial issues. (161)

82% of Londoners write letters. (176)

82% of British brides have a 'hen party'. (211)

82% of the British population said they had read a book in 1987. (233)

82% of Britons say they would not jump a queue. (259)

82% of British men clean their teeth before going to bed. (90)

82% of British couples have a honeymoon. (118)

**82% OF BRITISH PET OWNERS GRIEVE AS MUCH OVER THE LOSS OF A PET AS THEY DO OVER THE LOSS OF A MEMBER OF THE FAMILY. (74)**

For Gods sake Henry! Pass the dog!

DANGER QUICKSAND

# 83%

83% of British people feel that it is the government's responsibility to provide a decent standard of living for the unemployed. (35)

83% of British people agree that schools should teach children to obey authority. (35)

83% of British households have a telephone. (122)

83% of British homes with a garden have a lawnmower. (124)

83% of British women say they would never try whipping and sadism in the bedroom. (105)

83% of British housewives use self-raising flour. (131)

83% of Britons say they have never driven in the last 12 months while being over the limit. (208)

83% of British bridegrooms wear a wedding ring. (211)

83% of Britons think that judges should be able to give the death sentence in the case of murders of children. (231)

83% of Britons claim to dream at night. (230)

83% of British married women still masturbate. (105)

83.9% of Britons say that they don't like the idea of being in debt. (307)

83% of Britons judge doctors to be honest. (312)

**83% OF BRITISH WOMEN CLAIM THAT THEIR MEN MAKE IT PLAIN WHEN THEY ARE IN THE MOOD FOR PASSION. (276)**

# 84%

84% of British workers address each other by their Christian names. (285)

84 % of food advertising is aimed at women's press. (3)

84% of British 15–25-year-old males feel they might have sex outside marriage. (12)

84% of British women say their men are not prudish in bed. (85)

84% of British women say they know what all their bank charges are for. (114)

84% of British women who rate their sex lives as excellent or very good like fellatio. (105)

84% of British nurses disapprove of the idea of charging hospital patients for food. (344)

84.5% of British housewives never serve instant snack meals. (88)

84.5% of British adults buy chocolate bars. (88)

84.9% of British adults own a garden. (154)

84.3% of British housewives serve tomato ketchup. (88)

84% of Britons object to the live export of farm animals for slaughter in foreign abattoirs. (178)

84% of British motorists are in favour of automatic prison sentences for those convicted of a drink-driving offence where someone was killed or injured. (208)

84% of British women say they believe in staying loyal to their man. (332)

# 85%

85% of British women in Northern Ireland say their love lives are looking up. (82)

85% of British women in the North-East think their men's eyes are the sexiest around. (83)

85% of the British prison population in England and Wales are white. (120)

85% of British women say their men's behinds are just the way they like them. (83)

85% of British men take their partners out to dinner for a birthday treat. (86)

85% of British wives and girlfriends think they know exactly what their men earn. (87)

85% of British people favour a freeze on further nuclear weapon development. (95)

85.6% of the population of Great Britain live in England. (156)

Over 85% of British men lose their hair as they grow older. (212)

85% of British adults think that banks are well run. (227)

85% of British blood is Rhesus positive. (206)

85% of Britons think that the government should hold a referendum on capital punishment. (231)

85% of British women masturbate now. (105)

85.1% of British women buy tights and hold-ups. (88)

85% of Britons do not approve of schools teaching pupils that homosexuality is equal to heterosexuality. (315)

85% of British women who suffer premenstrual syndrome say they feel irritable at this time of the month. (149)

# 86%

86% of British people say they would never try 'wife swapping'. (105)

86% of British households have a colour television. (51)

86% of British people enjoy kissing on the lips. (89)

86% of British bridegrooms in the South wear a wedding ring. (118)

86% of British people feel that faithfulness is very important to a successful marriage. (35)

86.6% of British housewives use tea bags. (88)

86% of British people feel that parents should try to teach children honesty above all else. (35)

86% of British housewives use custard. (88)

86% of British people feel that the government should spend more on the Health Service, even if this means an increase in personal taxes. (132)

86% of British women say they have never been offered screening for breast cancer. (260)

86% of Britons do not know the role of the European Parliament. (190)

**86% OF BRITISH PEOPLE REGARD ACID RAIN AS A SERIOUS ENVIRONMENTAL HAZARD. (35)**

# 87%

87% of British 20–25-year-olds agree that success is a question of hard work. **(12)**

87% of British high earners (£25,000 + annual household income) are men. **(56)**

87% of British young women (aged 15–34 years) think more money should be spent on research into AIDS. **(76)**

87.5% of first-class letters posted in the United Kingdom are delivered by the next working day after collection. **(121)**

87% of people emigrating from the United Kingdom are under 45 years. **(127)**

87% of Britons do not know the name of their Euro MP. **(190)**

87% of British bridegrooms have a 'stag party'. **(211)**

87% of British 8–14-year-olds do not know what the Spanish Armada was. **(228)**

87% of British pub customers want pubs to open for four hours on Sunday lunchtimes. **(309)**

**88% OF THE BRITISH POPULATION DISAPPROVE OF THE IDEA OF SCRAPPING FREE DENTAL CHECKS. (137)**

# 88%

**88.5%** of British women use perfume or toilet water. **(88)**

**88.8%** of the British labour-force are in employment. **(155)**

**88%** of British teenagers are in favour of helping developing countries. **(167)**

**88% OF BRITISH URINALS SUFFER FAECAL CONTAMINATION. (45)**

# 89%

89.4% of British housewives serve sausages. (88)

89% of British men use a loofah. (90)

89% of British households still have a traditional Sunday lunch, the favourite being roast beef with Yorkshire pudding, roast potatoes, carrots and gravy followed by apple pie and custard. (111)

89% of Britons favour tougher gun laws. (194)

89% of British married people sleep in the same bed as their spouse. (230)

89% of British women over 60 years say they can reach multiple orgasms. (105)

89% of the British population disapprove of the idea of scrapping free eye tests. (137)

89% of Britons think that the Royal Family does a lot to promote Britain abroad. (277)

It's no use. I feel seasick

**89% OF BRITISH COUPLES SAY THEY WOULD TRY MAKING LOVE ON A WATERBED. (105)**

# 90%

90% of British people do not own a motorcycle. (10)

90% of British 15–25-year-olds feel it is wrong to be unfaithful to their partner. (12)

90% of British 15–25-year-olds feel strongly that condoms should be made more widely available. (12)

90% of British boys aged 17 regularly and illegally drink in pubs. (49)

90% of British 13–14-year-old boys spend between £30 and £40 per year on gambling. (13)

90% of British parents approve of their 15–19-year-old children having a steady friend of the opposite sex. (12)

90% of British people feel that waste from nuclear electricity stations has a serious effect on the environment. (35)

More than 90% of British school children have problems with their shoes or feet. (334)

Over 90% of British women do not want pictures of Page Three girls in their newspapers. (174)

90% of Scots look forward to Christmas. (204)

90% of British women who rate their sex lives as excellent or very good like cunnilingus. (105)

90% of British women would want to be told if they had a fatal illness. (255)

90% of British women say they vote in elections. (255)

90% of Scotsmen make their wives or girlfriends feel like the only woman in the world. (276)

90% of Britons who have bidets use them. (286)

Nearly 90% of Britons under 24 believe their partners have not been unfaithful. (287)

90% of migrants to the United Kingdom are under 45 years. (127)

# 91%

91% of British men know what their women earn. **(101)**

91% of British brides have had sexual relations with their fiancé before marriage. **(211)**

91% of British women say that men don't bother about contraception. **(332)**

91% of British employees say they 'understand' what is expected of them in their job. **(220)**

## 91% OF BRITISH MEN WOULD STOP TO HELP AN ANIMAL IN DISTRESS. (99)

# 92%

92% of British men use shampoo. (73)

92% of British housewives serve baked beans. (88)

92% of British people feel that marital violence is sufficient reason for divorce. (35)

92% of British housewives use floor and furniture polish. (88)

92% of British people think that there should be regular, mandatory eye tests for all drivers. (134)

92% of British husbands shopping alone usually use supermarkets. (144)

92% of Britons are in favour of compulsory wearing of rear seat-belts or child restraints by youngsters under 13 years old. (236)

92% of British women say that they are angry at being pressurized to have sex with a man on their first date. (332)

92% of Britons agree that all animals to be slaughtered for food should first be humanely stunned to prevent pain, no matter whether the meat is intended for Christians, Muslims or Jews. (178)

92% of British brides would mind if their fiancé saw their wedding dress before the day. (211)

92% of British households eat mushrooms at some time. (237)

92.4% of British women have masturbated at some time or other. (105)

92% of Britons expect a child to ask to leave the dining-table. (259)

92.8% of letters posted second class in Britain are delivered by the third day after posting. (291)

# 93%

93% of British households have an electric kettle. (40)

93% of British housewives serve bacon. (88)

93% of young British people vow they will never try heroin. (68)

93.4% of British adults drink alcohol. (88)

93% of Britons know of the existence of satellite television. (279)

93% of British women fill in their cheque-book stubs. (114)

93% of British people have never done anything to try to influence an Act of Parliament. (35)

93% of British MPs say that they receive mail from children of school age. (177)

93% of British women say that they have experienced fellatio. (105)

93% of British men shave every day. (274)

93% of British men are supportive, helpful and interested in their partner's job. (112)

# 94%

94% of British women say that they make the bed in the morning. **(285)**

94% of British drivers wear seatbelts. **(42)**

94% of British people over 55 years wear spectacles. **(134)**

94% of British men pay back on time money borrowed from a friend. **(86)**

94% of British men who have suffered from some form of worrying sexual advance or assault say it was from another man. **(238)**

94% of British women say they have experienced a sexual climax. **(105)**

94% of British women say they are happy about the size of their partner's sex organ. **(105)**

94% of Britons think standards of politeness are falling. **(259)**

94% of Britons say they always say 'good morning' to neighbours or work colleagues. **(259)**

94% of Britons think that the television should not remain on when guests arrive. **(259)**

Divorce! Why?

**94% OF BRITISH PEOPLE FEEL THAT CONSISTENT UNFAITHFULNESS IS SUFFICIENT REASON FOR DIVORCE. (35)**

# 95%

95% of British wine drinkers drink wine in their own home. (41)

95% of British brides say they made love with their fiancés before their wedding day. (118)

95% of the British population are white. (51)

95% of British employers notice whether a candidate for a job wears a tie. (272)

95% of British households have a refrigerator. (51)

95% of Britons say they welcome winter. (204)

95% of British brides wear a long dress on their wedding day. (211)

95% of British married men who are in unhappy relationships now believe that their sex education was inadequate. (238)

**95% OF BRITISH WOMEN SAY THAT THEIR MEN WOULD NEVER DREAM OF ASKING THEM, ON THEIR FIRST DATE, IF THEY HAD HERPES. (112)**

# 96% 97%

96.8% of British people in prison establishments in England and Wales are male. (42)

96% of British women read their bank statements. (114)

96% of British brides observe the tradition 'something old, something new, something borrowed, something blue'. (211)

96% of British women say that they have experienced cunnilingus. (105)

97% of British households do not own an electric footbath. (10)

97% of the white British population were born in the UK. (51)

97% of British households own a vacuum cleaner. (139)

97% of British households have a television. (164)

97% of British brides have bridesmaids or pageboys. (211)

**97% OF BRITISH BRIDES DISCUSS SEX WITH THEIR FIANCÉS.
(211)**

# 98% 99%

98% of British people feel it is the government's responsibility to provide a decent standard of living for the old. (35)

98% of British MPs say that people write appreciative letters to them. (177)

98% of British MPs strongly agree that letter-writing should continue to be taught as an important life skill. (177)

98% of Britons suffer from tooth decay. (225)

99% of British 15–25-year-old males feel it is wrong to use hard drugs. (12)

99.5% of conceptions in British women aged 13–15 were outside marriage. (17)

99% of live British babies are born in hospital. (42)

99% of British households have water heating. (139)

99% of Britons think that people should ask permisson to smoke in someone else's home. (259)

*Besides being strikingly handsome, I'm one of the 1% with healthy gums, look.*

**99% OF ADULTS IN THE UK ARE SUFFERING FROM GUM DISEASE. (224)**

# 100%

100% of London bankers and stockbrokers believe that ties are a very clear indication of a person's education and background. (272)

100% of British women whose partners have beards think they would look better clean-shaven in line with the current clean-cut image. (1)

100% of British 15–25-year-old females feel it is wrong to use hard drugs. (12)

**Virtually 100%** of British women over 60 years think it is morally OK to masturbate. (105)

100% of British men in Northern Ireland repay money borrowed from a friend...as soon as possible. (86)

100% of Britons eligible in 1984 for state retirement pensions and child benefits took them up. (263)

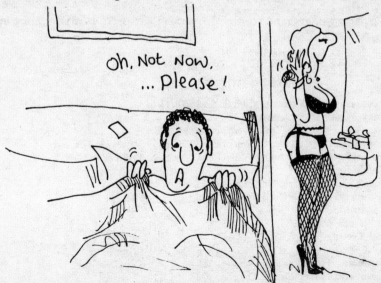

**100% OF BRITISH MEN WILL EXPERIENCE IMPOTENCE AT SOME TIME IN THEIR LIVES. (11)**

# SURVEY REFERENCES

1 – Wilkinson Sword Survey, 1987
2 – Youthscan UK 1987/**Sunday Times**, 22 November 1987
3 – Mirror Group Newspapers 'Shopping by Males'/MEAL, 1986
4 – Leisure Futures, Henley Centre/Marketing, 19 November 1987
5 – TUC Survey/**Daily Mail**, 17 November 1987
6 – Public Attitude Surveys Research/**The Times**, 20 November 1987
7 – 'Are you being served?'/Leo Burnett/Marketing, 19 November 1987
8 – Department of Transport/Paul Channon/Driving Test Arrangements, November 1987
9 – Gallup/**Daily Telegraph**, 11–16 November 1987
10 – BMRB/Mintel, 1987
11 – Marriage Guidance Council/**Today**, 18 November 1987
12 – McCann-Erickson Youth Study, 1987
13 – Exeter University/**Daily Telegraph**, 23 November 1987
14 – Mintel/Holiday Eating Habits 1987/**Today**, 18 November 1987
15 – Women's Health Today/Office of Health Economics, 1987
16 – Gallup Poll/**Daily Telegraph**, 21 November 1987
17 – **Social Trends** 17/CSO, 1987
18 – Pet Food Manufacturers Profile, 1987
19 – Mintel BMRB/Deodorants, 1987
20 – Mintel BMRB/Home Baking, 1987
21 – Mintel BMRB/Hotels, 1987
22 – Mintel BMRB/Bicycles, 1987
23 – Mintel BMRB/Children's Clothing, 1987
24 – Mintel BMRB/Cooled Storage Appliances, 1987
25 – Mintel BMRB/Chocolate Confectionery, 1987
26 – Mintel BMRB/Fish, 1987
27 – Mintel BMRB/DIY Chemicals, 1987
28 – Mintel BMRB/Domestic Lighting, 1987
29 – Mintel BMRB/Banking, 1987
30 – Management Today/ICL/**Daily Mail**, 1987
31 – British Airways, 1987
32 – The Business Woman's Travel Club Survey, 1987
33 – **Sunday Times**, 22 November, 1987
34 – Budget Rent a Car/**The Times**, 27 November, 1987
35 – **British Social Attitudes**, 1987/Social and Community Planning Research
36 – Literacy, Numeracy and Adults/ALBSU/MSC Research Project, 1987
37 – Bird's Eye Report, 1987
38 – Women's Health Today/Office of Health Economics, 1987
39 – Pet Protect/Gallup Poll/**Daily Mirror**, 9 November 1987
40 – The Swan 1986 Survey/Gallup
41 – Mintel BMRB/Wine, 1986
42 – **Social Trends**, 1987/CSO
43 – **Chief Executive Magazine**, 1987
44 – **Caterer and Hotelkeeper**, October 1987
45 – **Caterer and Hotelkeeper**, October 1987
46 – **Caterer and Hotelkeeper**, October 1987
47 – Calor Survey/**The Times**, 2 December 1987

**48** – **Woman's World**, December 1987
**49** – Young People in 1986/Health Education Survey
**50** – Barclaycard Survey, 1987
**51** – **General Household Survey**, 1986/OPCS Monitor
**52** – **She**/Motoring, September 1987
**53** – Family Expenditure Survey, 1986
**54** – What Next? Economic and Social Research Council/**Independent**, December 1987
**55** – Marplan/**Independent**/Channel 4, 3 December 1987
**56** – International Research Associates/NOP/Affluent Handbook, 1987
**57** – HMSO, 1987
**58** – Popular Foodservice/**Daily Telegraph**, November 1987
**59** – MORI/**The Times**, 3 December 1987
**60** – **Sunday Express** Survey, October 1987
**61** – Gallup/**Daily Telegraph**, 16 November 1987
**62** – **Daily Express**, 2 December 1987
**63** – **Daily Express**, 30 November 1987
**64** – Inside the Family/FPSC, 1987
**65** – **Independent**, 4 December 1987/Woolworth's
**66** – Social and Community Planning Research, 1987/**Standard**, 28 October 1987
**67** – **The Times**, 4 December 1987/Gallup Survey for TUC
**68** – **London Evening Standard**, 29 October 1987/Edwina Currie
**69** – **Today**, 3 December 1987
**70** – NOP/**Mail on Sunday**, 29 November 1987
**71** – Retail Business 346, December 1986/Economist Intelligence Unit
**72** – The Mail Order Industry/**The Times**, 25 January 1988
**73** – Retail Business 345, November 1986/Economist Intelligence Unit
**74** – Gallup/Pets Survey, October 1987
**75** – General Household Survey, 1984/OPCS
**76** – **19 Magazine**, October 1987
**77** – What's New in Marketing?, March 1987/Department of Employment, October 1986
**78** – What's New in Marketing?, April 1987/BMRB, 1986
**79** – The Polite Society/**Daily Mail**, 26 January 1988
**80** – **She**/NRS, 1986
**81** – **Vogue**/NRS, 1986
**82** – **Woman's World**, September 1987
**83** – **Woman's World**, August 1987
**84** – **Woman's World**, October 1987
**85** – **Woman's World**, November 1987
**86** – **Woman's World**, June 1987
**87** – **Woman's World**, July 1987
**88** – Target Group Index BMRB, 1987
**89** – **Daily Mail**/Gallup/Lypsyl Kissing Survey, 5 December 1987
**90** – **Woman's World**, April 1987
**91** – **Marketing Week**, 30 October 1987
**92** – **Pharmaceutical Journal**, November 1987
**93** – **Today**, 4 December 1987/OPCS
**94** – **Daily Telegraph**, 7 December 1987/Marplan/AA Foundation for Safety Research
**95** – **Guardian**, 7 December 1987/Reading University/Taylor Nelson Research
**96** – **Woman's World**, September 1986
**97** – **Woman's World**, November 1986

98 – **Woman's World**, October 1986
99 – **Woman's World**, January 1987
100 – **Woman's World**, March 1987
101 – **Woman's World**, February 1987
102 – **Woman's World**, December 1986
103 – **The Times**, 8 December 1987/MORI/NBC
104 – **Woman's World**, January 1986
105 – **She**, February 1987/Dr David Delvin/The Delvin Report on Safer Sex
106 – **Woman's World**, January 1986
107 – **Cosmopolitan**/Outline Low Fat Spread Survey, 1987
108 – **The Times**, 9 December 1987/Gallup
109 – The Beverage Report/Moccomat Ltd/Paragon Communications plc, 1987
110 – Dollond & Aitchison Group/Social Surveys (Gallup) Ltd, 1987
111 – Sharp Electronics (UK) Ltd/Gallup, 1987
112 – **Cosmopolitan**, 'What are men like today?', February 1987
113 – Polycell Report 1987/Taylor Nelson & Associates
114 – **Company**, September 1987
115 – **Company** GP Survey, October 1986
116 – Britain's New Abstinence, PAS Research Ltd/**The Times**, 10 December 1987
117 – BBC/Gallup/**The Times**, 10 December 1987
118 – **Wedding and Home** Marriage Survey, 1987
119 – **Options** Television Survey, December 1987
120 – **Social Trends** 17/Law Enforcement/CSO, 1987
121 – **Social Trends** 17/The Post Office, 1987
122 – **Social Trends** 17/British Telecom, 1987
123 – **Social Trends** 17/Ministry of Agriculture, Fisheries and Food, 1987
124 – Lawnmowers/BMRB, 1987
125 – **Social Trends** 17/NRS, 1985
126 – **Social Trends** 17/Labour Force Survey/Dept of Employment, 1985
127 – **Social Trends** 17/British Social Attitudes Survey, 1986
128 – **Social Trends** 17/Labour Force Survey/OPCS, 1987
129 – BARB, November 1987
130 – **Financial Times, 11 December 1987**/Conference Board of the US/AGB
131 – Flour Power - Gallup/Flour Advisory Bureau, 1987
132 – **Guardian**/Marplan NHS Poll, 11 December 1987
133 – Royal College of Nursing/**The Times**, 14 December 1987/Institute of Manpower Studies
134 – British American Optical/Gallup, 1987
135 – **Today**, 14 December 1987/Ratners/NOP
136 – ROSPA/Guide to Home Safety, 1987
137 – **Daily Telegraph**, 14 December 1987/Gallup
138 – NOP Financial Research Services, December 1987
139 – AGB Home Audit, 1986
140 – General Household Survey, 1982/HMSO, 1984
141 – Institute of Ophthalmology, 1987
142 – General Household Survey, 1981/HMSO, 1983
143 – BMRB/Proprietary Association of Great Britain/**Daily Mail**, 12 December 1987
144 – Mirror Group Newspapers (1986) Ltd/Shopping by Male
145 – **Look Now**, July 1987/Polaroid UK Ltd/NOP, January 1987
146 – **19 Magazine**, June 1987
147 – **Over 21**, July 1987/ Gallup

148 – **Over 21**, August 1987
149 – **Look Now**, February 1987/PMS Survey
150 – **Over 21**/Knickerbox Survey, April 1987
151 – Association of Market Survey Organisations/Audience Selection, December 1987
152 – **Chief Executive**, December 1987
153 – 1987 Realeat Survey/Gallup Poll
154 – Target Group Index, BMRB 1987
155 – **Employment Gazette**, HMSO 1987
156 – OPCS Population Trends, 1987
157 – OPCS Monitor, 1987
158 – Gallup International, 1986
159 – SMM & T, July 1987
160 – Allinson Breakfast Survey, 1987/ Biss Lancaster plc
161 – Marplan Royal Poll, December 1987
162 – Hoseasons The New Holiday Market/**Evening Standard**, 29 December 1987
163 – ITN/Marplan, December 1987
164 – Family Expenditure Survey 1986/**Guardian**, 31 December 1987
165 – Diamond Information Centre, 1987
166 – Gallup Poll Prospects for 1988/**Daily Telegraph**, 28 December 1987
167 – Third World Survey/**Guardian**, 30 December 1987
168 – Gallup/Church of England Clergy Survey/**Daily Telegraph**, 23 December 1987
169 – Professional Association of Teachers, December 1987
170 – **Best Magazine**, 21 October 1987
171 – Stress and the London Regional Transport Train Driver, 1987
172 – Concept Public Relations/Johnson and Johnson, June 1987
173 – News International/**Sun/Best Magazine**, September 1987
174 – **Best Magazine**, September 1987
175 – Everyday Health Care/BMRB, December 1987
176 – The Letter-writing Report, 1985/The Letter-writing Bureau
177 – The MP's Mail Bag 1986/The Letter-writing Bureau
178 – Compassion in World Farming/NOP, July 1987/**Guardian**, 8 October 1987
179 – Gallup/**Guardian**, 9 October 1987
180 – OPCS/**Guardian**, 23 September 1987
181 – Manchester University/**Guardian**, 16 September 1987
182 – Talk Back Poll/**Star**, 4 January 1988
183 – **Mail on Sunday**, 3 January 1988
184 – **Lancet/The Times**, 1 October 1987
185 – Inbucon Management Consultants Survey/**Today**, 7 October 1987
186 – The Restaurant Chain Index/**The Times**, 8 October 1987
187 – Press Association/**The Times**, 9 October 1987/**Guardian**, 9 October 1987
188 – Intervet UK Ltd/Pet Owners' Survey, 1987
189 – International Survey Research/**The Times**, 6 January 1988
190 – MORI/**Financial Times**, 6 January 1988/**Independent**, 6 January 1988
191 – MORI/Friends of the Earth/WWF/**Guardian**, 6 January 1988
192 – **Nursing Times/Today**, 1 January 1988
193 – CEGB/Dewe Rogerson Survey November 1987/**Financial Times**, 17 December 1987
194 – Facing South/**Daily Telegraph**, 9 October 1987
195 – Charities Aid Foundation/**Guardian**, 19 December 1987
196 – Labour Party/Comedia/**Guardian**, 4 January 1988
197 – Chief Executive Survey/**Daily Telegraph**, 4 January 1988

**198** – Guinness Survey, September 1987
**199** – Alcan Household Wraps Report, 1987
**200** – **Guardian**, 2 January 1988/Mintel
**201** – **Guardian**, 21 December 1987
**202** – Family Policy Studies Centre, Winter 1987/8 Bulletin
**203** – Bradford and Bingley Building Society/**Best Magazine**, 19 August 1987
**204** – Stone's Ginger Wine, Winter 1987 Report
**205** – British Videogram Association Gallup Survey/**Best Magazine**, August 1987
**206** – National Blood Transfusion Service, 1987
**207** – British Telecom Christmas Survey, 1987
**208** – Gallup Drink Driving Survey, November–December 1987
**209** – MORI/**The Times**, 4 January 1988
**210** – **Mail on Sunday**/NOP Poll, January 1988
**211** – **Brides and Setting Up Home**/Readership Survey, 1987
**212** – The Harley Dean Clinic Survey/**Best Magazine**, 28 October 1987
**213** – Management Incentive Schemes Survey/**The Times**, 23 December 1987
**214** – Institute of Directors/**The Times**, 10 December 1987
**215** – Schering Health Care Survey/**The Times**, 29 December 1987
**216** – Dr Ben Fletcher's London Cabbie Survey/**The Times**, 18 December 1987
**217** – **Daily Telegraph**, 30 December 1987
**218** – IBA – Behind and In Front of the Screen/**Best Magazine**, 8 November 1987
**219** – National Association of Gifted Children Survey/**Today**, 21 December 1987
**220** – ISR/**Financial Times**, 21 December 1987
**221** – **The Times**, 24 December 1987
**222** – **Journal of the Association of Sexual and Marital Therapists/The Times**, 8
January 1988
**223** – SMM & T/**Financial Times**, 8 January 1988
**224** – Wisdom Survey/Essentials, February 1988
**225** – **Daily Mail**, 7 January 1988
**226** – **Today** Survey, 7 January 1988
**227** – **New Society**/**The Times**, 8 January 1988
**228** – Marshall Cavendish/**Daily Telegraph**, 21 December 1987
**229** – **Family Circle** Feedback File, July 1986
**230** – The British Way Part II/**Daily Telegraph**/Gallup, November 1986
**231** – NOP Capital Punishment Survey, September–October 1987
**232** – ROSPA/The Facts about Accidents, December 1985
**233** – MORI/**Sunday Times**, 10 January 1988
**234** – MORI/**Sunday Times**, 10 January 1988
**235** – Bartlett & Co Insurance Survey/ **Independent**, 9 January 1988
**236** – Gallup/**Observer**, 10 January 1988
**237** – Mushroom Growers' Association, January 1988
**238** – Deirdre Sanders/The Woman Report on Men, 1987
**239** – Department of Employment Survey/**Daily Telegraph**, 7 January 1988
**240** – The Bathroom/BMRB, January 1988
**241** – **Guardian**/Marplan, 14 January 1988
**242** – The Sausage Report 1987/British Sausage Bureau
**243** – Wisdom Dental Survey, 1987
**244** – Channel 4 Survey/**Today**, 16 October 1987
**245** – **Slimming Magazine** Readers' Survey, 1987/8
**246** – **True Romances** Survey, 1987

**247** – **Guardian**/Marplan, 16 October 1987

**248** – **Guardian**/Marplan, 15 January 1988

**249** – NOP/BUPA/**Financial Times**, 15 January 1988

**250** – **Today**, 3 November 1987

**251** – **Guardian**, 9 January 1988

**252** – **Over 21** Fashion Survey, February 1988

**253** – **Woman**/ The Way We Are Survey, 14 November 1987

**254** – **Woman**/ The Way We Are Survey, 21 November 1987

**255** – **Woman**/ The Way We Are Survey, 28 November 1987

**256** – Prof. Cary Cooper/**Financial Times/ Guardian**, 8 January 1988

**257** – Michael Sullivan/**The Times**, 7 January 1988

**258** – NOP/**Daily Mail**, 14 October 1987

**259** – **Options** Opinion Manners Survey, February 1988

**260** – **Woman's Own** NHS Survey, 7 November 1987

**261** – Inland Revenue/**Guardian**, 13 January 1988

**262** – OPCS/**Daily Telegraph**, 13 January 1988

**263** – Social Trends No.18, 1988

**264** – Sketchley Dry-Cleaning Survey, January 1987

**265** – Home Office/Criminal Statistics England and Wales, 1986

**266** – OPCS, 1986

**267** – JICNARS/NRS, 1986

**268** – CACI Market Analysis, May 1987

**269** – **Family Circle**, 4 September 1985

**270** – Metropolitan Police Recruiting Centre, January 1988

**271** – UKCC, January 1988

**272** – The Tie Report, 1987/Munro & Forster PR for Tie Rack

**273** – The Addis Kitchen Report, February 1987

**274** – The Body Shop International plc, 1987

**275** – Race Relations in 1981/Commission for Racial Equality

**276** – **Woman's World**, February 1988

**277** – MORI/**Sunday Times**, 25 October 1987

**278** – **Consumer Voice**, 18 January 1988

**279** – Marketing Direction/Gallup/**Financial Times**, 18 January 1988

**280** – Marplan/**Guardian** 18 January 1988

**281** – Telephone Surveys Ltd/**Sunday Express**, 17 January 1988

**282** – NACRO/**Financial Times**, 18 January 1988

**283** – Gallup/Super Marketing, 15 January 1988

**284** – **Sunday Times**, 18 October 1987 Yershon Media

**285** – The British Way Part I/**Daily Telegraph**/Gallup, 17 November 1986

**286** – **Woman**, 23 May 1987/The Great British Bathroom Saga

**287** – Marplan/**Daily Express**/The British Way of Loving: Part I, 19 January 1988

**288** – Marplan/**Daily Express**/The British Way of Loving: Part II, 20 January 1988

**289** – Facts About Bread/Federation of Bakers, 1988

**290** – MORI/NCC/**Consumer Voice** , Summer 1987

**291** – Customer Audit and Review of the Post Office/**Consumer Voice**, Winter 1986

**292** – Consumer Dissatisfaction/OFT/**Consumer Voice**, Spring 1986

**293** – **Wedding and Home/Financial Times**, 20 January 1988

**294** – The Phobics Society, 1988

**295** – Racism Part I, **Sun**, Audience Selection Ltd 20 January 1988

**296** – **Today**, 20 January 1988

297 – Institute for Fiscal Studies/**Today**, 15 January 1988
298 – **Grocer**, 16 January 1988
299 – Radio 4, You and Yours/**Today**, 21 January 1988
300 – Racism Part II/**Sun**, 21 January 1988 Audience Selection
301 – Marplan/**Daily Express**/The British Way of Loving: Part III, 21 January 1988
302 – National Housing & Town Planning Council/**Independent**, 21 January 1988
303 – AMDA/**Financial Times**, 18 January 1988
304 – Gallup/**Daily Telegraph**, 21 January 1988
305 – Gallup/**Best Magazine**, 13 December 1987
306 – Target Group Index/BMRB, 1986
307 – Target Group Index/Life Style, BMRB, 1987
308 – Management Horizons/DIY Shopping/**Marketing Week**, 8 January 1988
309 – Clifton Inns/**Daily Express**, 13 January 1988
310 – British Cardiac Society/**Daily Express**, 13 January 1988
311 – Horack & Associates/**Independent**, 22 January 1988
312 – Market Research Society/**The Times**, 22 January 1988
313 – Market Research Society/**Independent,** 22 January 1988
314 – Gallup/FDS/**Daily Telegraph**, 22 January 1988
315 – Harris/**Daily Mail**, 25 January 1988
316 – Labour Research Department/**Ms London**, 25 January 1988
317 – **Mail on Sunday**, 24 January 1988
318 – Gallup/**Observer**, 24 January 1988
319 – **Woman's Own**, 30 January 1988
320 – Gallup/**Daily Telegraph**, 25 January 1988
321 – Gallup/**Daily Telegraph**, 23 January 1988
322 – Crystal Holiday Villas/The British Abroad/**Independent**, 25 January 1988
323 – MORI/**The Times**, 25 January 1988
324 – Halifax Building Society/**Daily Mail**, 25 January 1988
325 – Lifestyle Mintel/**Marketing**, 28 January 1988
326 – Channel 4/**Marketing**, 22 October 1987
327 – Gallup, August 1987
328 – IBA/**The Times** 29 January 1988
329 – RoSPA/**Daily Telegraph** 29 January 1988
330 – Young Guardian/Carrick James Opinion Poll 17 February 1988
331 – **Marketing** 11 February 1988
332 – **Woman's Own/Daily Mail** 15 February 1988
333 – **Woman's World/Guardian** 9 January 1988
334 – **The Times** 16 February 1988
335 – **The Times** 9 February 1988
336 – **Marplan/The Guardian** 9 February 1988
337 – Marriage Guidance Council/**Today** 10 February 1988
338 – Autosheen Survey/**Independent** 10 February 1988
339 – Gallup/**Independent** 10 February 1988
340 – Russell Harty's Notebook/**Sunday Times** 14 February 1988
341 – Harris Research Centre/**The Times** 15 February 1988
342 – **Mail on Sunday Magazine** 7 February 1988
343 – Gallup/**Sunday Telegraph** 7 February 1988
344 – MORI/**The Times** 2 February 1988
345 – **Super Marketing** 29 January 1988
346 – Gallup/UFO Research Association/**Guardian** 17 February 1988